How Our Children with Autism Raised Us as Parents

The Ninety-Nine Jobs Needed to Raise Kids with Autism

by Sandy Hallett, Nikki Wisor

RoseDog Books

PITTSBURGH, PENNSYLVANIA 15222

LSTA Autism Grant

ISBN: 978-1-4349-9514-8
Printed in the United States of America

First Printing

For more information or to order additional books,
please contact:
RoseDog Books
701 Smithfield Street
Pittsburgh, Pennsylvania 15222
U.S.A.
1-800-834-1803
www.rosedogbookstore.com

To our husbands who help us to keep our sense of humor and sanity; to our children who make each day a new and exciting journey; and to our family and friends who love us and help support us when we need it most.

To a special little boy, Marcus, who overwhelmingly touched our hearts. We know you never stood a chance but you are in a better place.

Acknowledgments

Although Sandy Hallett and Nikki Wisor wrote this book, countless people had a hand in helping with the stories and information in it. To our families, the constant love and support you give us is more than we could ever ask for. Our friends are also a big part of the book. Thanks to Lenny and Holly for your support of Ryan and your encouragement for getting me to put my thoughts on paper. This was the first obstacle I needed to overcome. Once those floodgates opened, the rest was history. Thanks Sheila for your daily phone updates to Nikki and I, to make sure we're sane. Thanks to Jenny for your open ear and your constant "fun making". To Danielle, my "Ambassador of Kwan." For your encouragement, real estate expertise and support in helping to get this project to the publisher. The girls' from Perrysburg, for all their countless years of unconditional love, and for Jo Mama, for keeping my bucket full and undertaking the great job of editing this two year project! Thanks to Nikki especially, for finishing my sentences by the time we were done with this project and because we understand what the daily routines entail. There are so many other friends to mention, but that will have to be in the sequel. As far as our advocates and doctors, thanks Dr. Mark Deis- our guru and personal physician of all 5 children and Dr. Patricia Manning- Courtney of Children's Hospital in Cincinnati. She works in the Kelly O'Leary center and has been a great help to us, too.

We of course have to acknowledge the kids' schools. Ryan attends the Seneca County Opportunity School in Tiffin, Ohio. Thanks to Val, Deb, Sally, Brett, Kathy and Rachel and everyone else at the school. They have been huge advocates for Ryan and children with autism in Tiffin. Both schools taught Ryan to sign his name and shake his head in decision. Who knew? - And Lew, thanks for all you do, too!

At Goodridge Elementary where T.C. and Sean had been in the same class for three years, we want to thank Mrs. Amanda Stone, and of course Mrs. Ellen Grimme. Our families have met so many therapists, too. Thank you all for your tireless hours to help our kids!

Introduction

Thank you for picking up this book and reading it. By choosing this book you probably know someone with autism. With the statistics of one in one hundred fifty children being diagnosed with autism, most people know someone on the autism spectrum. Why did Nikki and I write this book? We're two moms with five kids, four on the autism spectrum, who have read a lot of books regarding the subject of autism. The books were informative, but somewhat discouraging and depressing. This book is a collaboration of two moms with four kids on the autism spectrum with the same sense of purpose, similar interests and sense of humor. Our shared perspectives are from a more optimistic point of view. Autism is a life sentence and it should be embraced. We have become better people, better friends and especially better parents because of what all of our children have taught us.

Now, let me introduce my family and myself. I'm Sandy Hallett. Twenty years ago I was a student at Kent State University in Kent, Ohio. I was attending an eleven-keg party where I met the love of my life, Mike Hallett. I was a swimmer at Kent State and he was a football player at Kent State, and later at Mount Union College.

From across the courtyard, our eyes met and we fell instantly in love. Yea right. It did take us a *long* three weeks before he proposed and we were engaged.

We have been blessed with two beautiful boys. Theiler Christian (sounds like Tyler and is my mother's maiden name). Theiler, T.C., as we like to call him, is nine years old. You see, my parents put an old, ancient curse on me when I was young. I was to give birth to a child and have him grow up to look, act and be just like me. Bingo, meet my oldest son T.C. He is a loving, sweet, sensitive boy, a great big brother and he has a silver, sarcastic tongue like his mother. I guess I deserved that one!

The other beautiful boy in my life is Ryan. He is our son with autism. He is eight years old and the spitting image- "mini me" of my husband, Mike. He is laid back in personality and doesn't' communicate very much. That's not because he has autism and he's non-verbal, I think it's just because he's a guy and he'll speak when he's ready! T.C. and Ryan are my "Irish twins" at fifteen months apart in age. They are both very similar and different in so many ways, just as all siblings are, regardless of special needs. They are the best of friends and worst of enemies, emotions changing on a dime with no notice. I will say though, when T.C. walks in a room, Ryan's baby blues light up like they do for no one else!

We, the Hallett family, live in a small, charming town in Northwest Ohio named Tiffin, Ohio. Mike is the head football coach at Heidelberg University. We have lived here almost two years after residing for eight years in Northern Kentucky where Mike previously coached at Thomas More College. Mike's passion is football and his family. My passion is people. I'm passionate about my family and people; I'm passionate about my friends and people; I'm passionate about entertaining with people. People. People. People.

I'm Nikki Wisor. I was born in Philadelphia and grew up in the suburbs. I met my husband, Steve, in 1992 while we were students at Penn State University. We met at a party hosted by his fraternity, we fell in love and the rest is history. We were married in 1995.

In 1999 Sean was born. We knew from the beginning he was something special. The minute he was born and they weighed him, he broke the scale! He hasn't been able to fit into a typical standard ever since. Sean is extremely intelligent, loving and he has a great sense of humor. He is a whiz with computers and like any other nine-year-old boy, he enjoys his video games. He is not only gifted in music but he enjoys it thoroughly. Geography, reading and math are his favorite subjects in school.

My daughter Caley, is the child that my mother wished upon me! Not only is she my spitting image, she behaves the same way I did as a child. She is sweet and loving one minute- then look out, she may turn on you. My mother had a saying: "I would wake up in the morning with my horns twisted." I never fully understood what that meant until I had Caley. Her stubbornness is second only to her father. This trait she inherited I hope will only make her a stronger person. She is very generous with her friends and siblings, but like any child, she does revel in the torture of her siblings, too. Her hobbies include bike riding, playing with dolls, she loves to play outside and her favorite pass time is playing video games with her dad.

Caley's situation is unique. She is the middle child, but she functions as the oldest child in terms of her role in the family. She is very protective of Sean and Kiera. Her position on the autism spectrum is not as severe as her older brother, Sean, so we tend to expect more out of her.

Our youngest, Kiera, is a combination of both Sean and Caley. She is our "little sunshine." Our decision to have a third child may have been a result of Sean's diagnosis of autism and Caley's developmental delay. Who would take care of them both when we're gone?

Kiera is very artistic. She loves to paint, color and especially take photographs. She is an aspiring photographer! Like her mother, she also likes tiny toys. I had a dollhouse as a child that my father built me and Kiera enjoys the same miniature toys. She is also my animal lover. She adores anything with four feet and fur- the taller the better.

I think living in Kentucky, away from our families, has made us an unusually close- knit family. We may understand our children, or are more "in tune" with our children, than other families. Steve and I would rather spend twenty-four/seven with the kids than do anything else.

We don't enjoy anything as much as spending time with our children.

Contents

This book is hopefully part education, part inspiration, part reality and a little comic relief to top it off. Most, if not all people can relate to the stories in these pages, whether you have a typical or atypical child. It's really how you take in life when it's handed to you and how you deal with certain situations. No two parents are alike just like no two children with special needs or autism are the same. That is why Nikki and I thought some stories of our four kids, all falling on various degrees of the Autism Spectrum and our typical kids, will give you perspective on how different people cope with different situations. What is that saying? "When life gives you lemons, make lemonade." We have a lifetime supply of lemonade! Now it may be organic, sugar free, diet lemonade, with additives, preservatives and some medicine or supplements in it, but lemonade all the same. Sure, some days are harder than others, but let's be realistic. You have your good days and bad days too. We just happen to add a little goofiness or sarcasm to each situation (which is totally lost on a child with autism so I don't recommend it or understand why I continue to speak to them like that!)

We decided to write this book to shed some light (and / or insight) on the lighter side of Autism. And YES there is . . . (a lighter side that is). We have read hundreds of books, thousands of articles and e-mails; we've gone to meetings, conferences, and support groups and each have at least five autism magazine subscriptions. Some have been helpful and informative; however they are also extremely depressing. Autism is not a death (or life) sentence. There's a lighter side to everything. It's all in how you look at it, right? Is your glass half empty or half full? Sandy mentioned making lemonade out of lemons, I say let's make margaritas!!! Let's enjoy the roller coaster ride with our children. Have you ever just sat on the floor and spun the wheel to a matchbox car for two minutes? It clears the mind and clutter in the brain- and it's pretty relaxing. If it's true that "laughter" is the best medicine, than I say we should open a comedy club. Some days if we don't laugh, we'll cry. Yes, we have bad days, who doesn't? These are the cards we were dealt. Do we bluff, bet, or fold? We have wonderful, beautiful, caring children and we are so lucky to have them all! They are only babies for a short time. I read an article once, where the author quoted a needlepoint that her grandmother made. I was so moved I've forgotten all but the last few lines...

"...Dust bunnies go away
For I haven't time to sweep.
I'm raising my babies,
And babies don't keep."

We'll do anything to help our babies; why else would we hang a swing in our living room or put our computer on the coffee table...so my son can sit on a potty seat chair while playing on the computer, why else? I'm not sure if it's all about how much you know. It's about how much you care. By being well educated, strong and funny we are giving our kids the best we can. They deserve the best parents; after all, we were chosen to be a parent of special needs children, so that makes us special, too. We're not perfect Mom's, just Mom's who care. We make mistakes...plenty of them. There really aren't handbooks on what to do when your child_____, Hey maybe that should be our next book! Don't get me wrong, read all the information about autism you can get your hands on, but take it all with a grain of salt, you know, for the margaritas.

There may come that day when you first realize something may be a little "off" or "askew" with your child. You continue down that path until you finally realize there is an issue. You may then seek a medical professional's opinion to get a formal diagnosis and find special services. After these realizations you find there are many great resources at hand, but you may not know where to start looking. The Internet is a start for information. Friends who know someone with a child with special needs, support groups, and reading books can also help. After my son started showing signs of autism at two years old and was diagnosed with autism at two and a half, I became a voracious reader. Of course I could barely finish a book because I became so depressed. When your child is diagnosed you want to know the future isn't as bleak as it seems. Most books out there are a "cornucopia" of facts but they tend to make you a little sad. Let's face it; if you have a child with autism, you need to have time for research and time for grieving for the uncertainty of their future. We don't know what the future holds as far as research is concerned. Each year we seem to get a little closer to possible answers to the puzzle named autism, or just at peace with the cards we were dealt. All I know is when my son was diagnosed with autism, he wouldn't look me in the face and the light behind his eyes was gone. Three years later the gleam is back in his eyes followed by a big dimply grin. He appears to have a quality of life and a happiness that some people may never experience. Isn't that all we really want for our children, is for them to be happy? Some people have all the money in the world and my not reach that sense of innocence and peace that he appears to have. He cries like any other child but the amount of laughter definitely outweighs the crying. Maybe a little whining too, but we all do that! Of course if I could trade places with him for 1 day, or have him tell me how he feels, than that story may not ring true. For now, though, that's my story and I'm sticking to it!

There are so many hats you need to wear as a parent of a child with special needs; we thought it only appropriate to take our top ninety-nine jobs needed for raising a child with autism. The definitions may be altered from Webster-Merriman's accurate portrayal with our own spice added, but the stories will ring true with most of you. Hopefully there are some facts to be sifted though and some laughs to be made as you filter through our experiences. Obviously our portrayal of the occupations versus the real definition may vary. One thing is clear. Through our personal journaling and writing of this book, we have learned so many things as parents that our children have taught us. I know the Hallett's and the Wisor's have all become more patient, forgiving and loving parents after being chosen as parents of children with special needs.

Nikki Wisor and Sandy Hallett, 2007

1. Parent

One that begets or brings forth offspring/ a person who brings up and cares for another. (Dictionary Version)

SANDY: Fair, Firm and Friendly. I remember hearing those words at my Father-in- laws funeral. As far as parenting tips go I remembered them. You want to try and be fair to your children. It is a hard line with a typical and an atypical child. T.C., my nine year old, is always trying to be a parent to Ryan. I don't want T.C. to grow up too fast just because his little brother has some limitations. Being fair can be a complicated balancing act too, because the typical child may sometimes perceive the special needs child as getting more attention. It's really not more or less attention, just different attention. You also need to be firm. There have to be boundaries, and rules need to be set for both children. The degrees may vary, though. After setting boundaries follow through is important. If you tell them to do something, no matter how hard it is, stick to your guns. Boundaries are very important! After setting the boundaries and following through you want to be friendly. You want to be friendly with your kids, just not their best friend. I like being a parent. It kind of snuck up on me and surprised me. We were late bloomers with our child rearing. Before my thirtieth birthday I gave birth to T.C. I haven't always been the maternal, nurturing type of person, so my husband tells me he was pleasantly surprised by my mothering ability. What did he think I was going to do? I guess I was trying to become a knowledgeable, mature, and tolerant adult before raising my own kids. Well anyone that knows me knows I threw all caution to the wind because I have none of those traits! My secret to being a parent is to be at their level. Not on purpose, of course. It's because I have been living my forty years perpetually as a ten year old. I like to go to the park or play ball in the back with my kids. I also like to take them swimming at the YMCA. At the pool the other day T.C. said his nose was running. What would a ten year old say? "If it's running you better go catch it!" He had to hold his stomach he was laughing so hard. The problem is, my entire playground "comebacks" are at a second grade level. Eventually I am going

1

to need some new material. Who else hears something like: "I love spinach quiche" and my witty retort is "Why don't you marry it?" You see where I'm going with this. I think as parents our sense of humor helps in a lot of situations that need some levity. My husband is an amazing parent. He gets right down on the floor with the boys. Nothing is funnier than watching a six foot six inch, three hundred twenty pound, college football coach dancing and singing to the kid's group "the Wiggles" with our kids! As a coach you would think sports and big masculine boys would be his aspirations for his children. He always said, " Just so they are happy and good at something they love, I would be a proud Father. It doesn't have to be football or baseball. It can be art, or sports or music. Anything, as long as they're happy!"

I just had a huge day recently as a parent! Ryan had a couple of tough, emotional days. My husband had recently taken a new job at a different college and the boys' and I stayed behind to sell the house. Ryan, who is non-verbal, has a hard time expressing his feelings unless he is sad or frustrated. That day at school he appeared very agitated and was pinching a few kids. Ryan pinches to express himself or when he is out of this element. The teacher's tried to figure out his frustrations, but they couldn't. Finally, Ryan went over to his communication device and hit the icon button for "bad day". That was a HUGE breakthrough for us, because he is just learning how to use the device. He could usually express food needs, but not necessarily a certain emotion. The next day he was equally emotional but he just seemed sad. When he got home from school he had respite care. Respite care is when you have someone come into your home and watch your child so you can get a little time off for yourself. There is either in home or respite care where you drop your child off with a caregiver. His respite caregiver told me after I left he became more sad. When she hugged him and asked him what was wrong, he took her by the hand and walked with her over to a photograph of Ryan and me and pointed to it. We believe he was telling her he missed me! I have never heard my son say my name before and that breaks my heart. For him to point to my picture, or to sign "mommy" that melts my heart like nothing else!

NIKKI: I've been told I have the patience of a saint or Jobe. I can wait out most temper tantrums, (even my husband's) kids screaming, pinching, kicking and other behavioral issues that most parents and grandparents have mentioned a good smack would help. I usually take a deep breath, ask GOD for patience, sigh and know it will get better.

My husband is such a kid himself, no one notices our children are different at the playground, because of the crazy man running around screaming. He raises the bar and makes most Moms' jealous that their husbands don't play with their children like that. He screams, yells, and he runs up and down the slide. He re-enacts

The Hallett Family Portrait taken at Aunt Jo's house in 2004

Dr. Seuss the "star bellied sneetch machine"- in again, out again. He does this as he chases the kids around the jungle gyms and slide. They squeal with delight! He gets quite a work out too!

I'm always amazed when parents (usually Moms) say things to me like "I can't believe you're letting him/her play in the sandbox? It's so dirty!" Gee really? I hadn't noticed. Sand, dirt, mud- what's the difference? At least it is not poop! Kiera is always my biggest gamble when she plays in the sandbox. I have to watch her like a hawk!!!! This is because she will eat everything- literally. Can you say toxoplasmosis? Sean and Caley are usually pretty good about not eating sand, and who cares if they get dirty. Caley throws a bit more sand than I like, but what's the point of going to the playground if not to PLAY? Come on it's in the name!

When I was a kid, and even while pregnant with Sean, I imagined what it would be like to be a parent. It was nothing like what I do now. I dreamed of ballet, dance lessons, school plays, hockey practice, ice skating lessons, piano lessons, swim team practice, gymnastics, cub scouts/girl scouts, bake sales, being room mother and cheerleading practice. I also envisioned dressing my girls up in fancy girly clothes, fixing their hair and painting their finger and toenails. Yes, I think I always knew I'd have girls. My life now consists of physical therapy, speech therapy, developmental interventionists, behavior therapy and occupational therapy. I didn't even know what an occupational therapist was until I needed one. In case you were wondering, occupational therapist's work on fine motor skills and physical therapist's work on gross motor skills. I never knew what a citizen's advocate was either until we had to sit down and do an IEP (Individual Education Plan.) with the school and administrators. It's amazing the amount of information I've learned out of pure necessity. I've also learned about hippo therapy. No, surprisingly not riding on hippos, its therapeutic horseback riding. Furthermore there are art and music therapies we haven't tried yet. I have also recently looked into getting an autism awareness "service" dog for Sean. These dogs are trained to learn each child's individual needs and personality. In Sean's case, the dog would be with him one hundred percent of the time, even at school. The dog would alert us if he was trying to get out of the house, or God forbid if he got out of the house or school without our knowledge, the dog would stay with him until we found him. These dogs cost approximately twenty thousand dollars. Pocket change, right? Besides the financial commitment, there are also special weekly and monthly training sessions required for keeping the dog focused on his job. I've spoken to several parents of children with autism who have these magnificent dogs and they recommended having a family dog as well. The reasons they gave was that if you have typical children in the house and they play or pay more attention to the dog, the dog will get distracted and be less effective.

Some days are harder than others when parenting special needs children, but I learn something new from them every day. They can always make me laugh and they love with their whole being. I would never trade them for the world. I would like to change the way the world sees them and somehow shelter them from anything bad that may come. What parent wouldn't?

4

Steve with Sean, Caley and Kiera Wisor at Christmas in 2007

2. Music Teacher

One whose occupation is to instruct the science or art of ordering tones or sounds in succession, in combination, and in temporal relationships to produce a composition having unity and continuity. (Dictionary Version)

SANDY: Whether it is pots and pans, musical toys, CD's or some other form of music, many kids with autism have some connection to music. We take a lot of road trips since we are not from the Northern Kentucky area. Since we are not originally from the area, my children are used to taking long trips in the car, listening to various forms of music. Part of the problem with that is I am what you would call a heavy metal "head banger." I like my heavy rock and roll music. I choose to listen to various rock groups like Metallica, Godsmack, GreenDay and Nickelback. It is pretty cool when your kids can sing a long, but even I know a good range of music will probably be better in the end for growing minds. Living in Kentucky, country music is popular. Both kids seem to respond to Country. I can only listen to it in smaller doses, though. Baby Steps. We listen to classical music, 60's, 70's, 80's and oldies. My son T.C. does a mean Elvis Presley impersonation. We have many soundtracks the kids are familiar with, too. The Lion King, Toy Story, and Baby Einstein CD's are some of our collection. When the kids were young they loved those "Kidz Bop" CD's! In the winter, right after Ryan was diagnosed with autism, he and I drove nine hours to a D.A.N. physician in Richmond, Virginia. (Readers digest version: D.A.N. stands for defeat autism now. There is a protocol related to D.A.N. The doctors do biological testing with results that can help treat the symptoms some children with autism may have. Issues with these children may be, but are not limited to, a genetic predisposition toward food allergies, treating an unusual response to a viral load such as vaccines that may trigger an abnormal immune response or an illness as a by product to antibiotics or a "leaky gut". Most children with autism never have formed stools.) Now, back to the subject at hand. Since my son is non-verbal you can understand the lack of conversation between he and I, so music was the common thread we enjoyed together. We did a lot of singing! To this day that memory of mine is probably on of the best I had with Ryan. I learned a lot about autism but I also learned a lot about Ryan, too. He couldn't sing with me in a conventional way but the way he listens to music and the way it makes him seem-well; his love and appreciation for music is contagious.

The newest addition to the kid's favorite toys is their new MP3 players they received for Christmas. They sit for hours and have their own personal jam sessions. What took us so long to figure that one out!

NIKKI: I grew up on music. My parents were always playing musical albums (yes, I'm that old) on the record player like Fiddler on the Roof, West Side Story, Sound of Music and who could forget Sundays with Sinatra, Frank of course with Syd Mark, (who if I'm not mistaken also has a grandson with autism?) I still remember the thrill of learning how to play an instrument with my first music teacher in grade school, Miss Toni Carmosa, at Inglewood Elementary School in Lansdale, Pennsylvania. My piano teacher, Frank Bartholomew, God rest his soul, seemed to enjoy torturing me and making me play Fur Elyse by Beethoven approximately a gazillion times. Remember that guy on Sesame Street that would bang his head on the piano when he messed up? Well I kept waiting for Mr. Bartholomew to do that every time I played the wrong notes, but he never did.

The kids love hearing and playing music too. Sean has perfect pitch. It's so perfect that when he hears bad music tones from certain toys or our wonderful relatives who sing off key, it would make his eyes well up with tears. The "Happy Birthday" song was literally painful for him to hear from his first Birthday. At age three, Sean taught himself how to play "Twinkle, Twinkle, Little Star" on the keyboard in his bedroom, and then on his xylophone. Correctly too!!! No, he doesn't know how to read music, but he naturally has an ear for music. When he was very young, I took him into a store in the mall. There was a music box he was listening to. Before I knew it, there were tears streaming down his face because of the sound. I was heartbroken. When his sister Caley was an infant and she would cry, that would make his ears hurt, too. It was very sad to watch.

Caley, unfortunately is a bit tone deaf, and she likes to sing all of the time. It makes her happy! As an added bonus, it drives Sean crazy so she sings even louder and with more frequency! Kiera doesn't speak much, and is just learning how to sing and dance. She is too young for us to tell if she's tone deaf or has perfect pitch, yet. My husband Steve and I love music, so we play it all of the time. We both sang in chorus and choir at school and church when we were younger. Right now Kiera sings more than she talks and Sean is starting to learn about harmony. We love harmonies, too. Steve and I are both pretty strong singers and I think we're pretty good. That's all that matters. Anyway, Sean plays songs over and over (and over and over . . .) He plays songs thousands of times just to learn the notes and learn how to sing them. At one point we talked about guitar or keyboard lessons (because who can afford a piano). Of course when would we fit in the time?

Sean amazes me. For a kid who does not like noise, he still takes all of the pots and pans in the kitchen and plays the drums with them. I don't know any famous drummers but I'm sure he can compare in stamina. His jam sessions usually last approximately twenty minutes or so. That is until Caley joins in. My brother-in-law, Scott, has a drum kit. He has a practice drum, which is silent (Thank God!) He brought it up to show Caley how to play the drums. She then played the drums, naked, standing on the table. She looked like a natural too. We're hoping this isn't a future profession? OK, at least not the naked part. I am just happy we have a love and appreciation of music. We are so lucky to have a common thread. Not all families do.

Caley blowing the trumpet with her friends Landen and Skye, 2007

3. Librarian

A specialist in the care or management of a library; a place in which literary, musical, artistic, or reference materials (as books, manuscripts, recordings, or films) are kept. (Dictionary Version)

SANDY: After we moved into our house in Kentucky we decided the formal dining room was a waste of space, so we made it into a den. We have a lot of books. Our collection consists of sport books, kid's books, self-help books and or course books on autism. I was an art history major at Kent State University back in the ninety's. You know all of those beautiful coffee table art books you see? Well that's also part of our book collection. We've moved those beautiful books twelve times in our fourteen years of marriage. They sure are pretty, but they are really heavy. Mike is not a fan!!! Every time we move them he asks me how many times I have read those books in the last decade. Good question! Most of our books came with book jackets. Well at least they started with book jackets. The book jackets only last approximately one day. Ryan likes to take the book jackets off, so he can tear them into little pieces. He got into a phase where all of the books on the shelves needed to be taken out of the bookcases and thrown on the floor for some reason. That drove me crazy! I couldn't tell if it was because he needed chaos in his orderly life? On any given day, I would clean up the den numerous times. I would leave for a couple of minutes, come back, and all of the books would be thrown on the floor. I would clean up the books, move onto another task, come back, and the books were all over the floor . . . again. Yet I would continually pick them up. Move them to a higher level? Put them away? No, I didn't even think of that.

NIKKI: What is it about the library that makes my kids have to poop? Every time we go, at least one of the kids has to go number two. I'm not sure if it's the quiet, the concentration, the relaxation, or just some fine reading. We have had some trouble getting Sean potty trained, maybe if we just drop a toilet in the library?

Sean likes to line up books that are similar. He'll line up all the same books by size, by the same publisher, or all by author. It makes sense to him. For years, he took every book off of his shelves and would sit and read them. It drove me crazy! I even put them in a box as a punishment for making such a mess. Who in their right mind takes books away as a punishment? Hey, I never claimed to be in my right mind. Why are books better when they are sprawled all over the floor? He does similar things at bookstores and libraries too, so we don't go to either very often. I fully understand what the librarians go through after we leave. Caley used to eat books and now Kiera has picked up the habit, so we've reduced the visits to the library. I could open a bookstore with the multiple books and bookshelves we have in our home. I'm sure it's in the thousands. Steve says I have turned the Dewey Decimal System into the Screwy All Messed Up System. No system whatsoever, but I can usually find whatever book is being asked for.

When we do go to the library, I appreciate how great the librarians are at our local library. I love that they have children's reading hour and playtimes. It is great for social interactions without too much structure or judgments from bystanders. The librarians know what to expect when they see us coming and they are always smiling and know us by name. Thank you Miss Karen's for always being so friendly, caring, and helpful. It's very nice to go somewhere where we can be ourselves without the dirty looks.

4. Warden

A person charged with the care or custody of persons, animals, or things; keeper. (Dictionary Version)

SANDY: By the end of the day my patience is done. After working all day and listening to Ryan pace by the refrigerator, looking for his next meal, for three hours at night, I can't take it any more! Every day around four o'clock p.m. we would go to the YMCA. That is because Ryan and I definitely need it for our sensory and weight issues! I dropped the kids in the child watch for about a half hour, I worked out and then I would go get them. We all swam for another half hour; we shower and then go home for dinner. By seven o'clock p.m. at night, it is time for lockdown. The special door chimes are activated and the extra locks on the top of the doors are switched over. I make T.C. finish his homework, they brush their teeth, take a bath and then I turn off the lights. I go and find the magic potion in the cupboard. It is called melatonin. Some children, especially kids on the autism spectrum, do not naturally produce enough melatonin in their brain so they do not get to sleep easily, or they do not stay asleep. We buy the melatonin supplements over the counter and it aids Ryan with his sleep patterns. I would give Ryan three milligrams of melatonin around eight o'clock p.m. and he falls asleep about a half hour later. On school nights, T.C. also goes to bed around eight thirty p.m. Now it's one of my favorite times of the day, LIGHTS OUT! Ok, slight exaggeration. I love spending time with the kids, but after a long day, I need some down time too. I know, it's all about me, right? At the end of the day, we sit together on the couch together, we may read, watch TV or just snuggle. There is nothing better than two kids falling asleep against me. They have those little angel faces when they sleep! It puts the day in perspective when you watch them sleeping peacefully. After I take them to bed I check the locks again.

NIKKI: At our house we have had to install nails in the sliding glass doors to keep the kids in. We also have magnetic alarms on the doors, and a chain lock we installed

11

on the door leading to the garage. The front door has a hotel lock on it. Previous deterrents were jingle bells, wind chimes, and those plastic safety doorknob covers, which Sean defeated by age three. We also have the hinge locks. We installed heavy suction cups on the windows so if the windows are lifted up more than an inch it will stop them. I have PVC pipes standing up in the window frame as a back up to the suction cups. If all else fails it will make some noise. We applied for a State funded grant to install a fence in our backyard for safety reasons. Behind our fence we have a retention pond. For those of you who don't know the number 1 cause of death for children with autism is drowning.

Kiera's guardian angel was working overtime last winter. I let the kids into the house after grocery shopping, and I went back out to the car to grab another bag. In that amount of time, I heard Kiera crying, like she was outside. When I got back inside I saw the sliding glass door wide open. Sean had taken the nail out of the back door (Thanks Uncle Chris for your invention, it usually works) leading to our second story deck outside of the kitchen. It was icy and I found her, barefoot, at the bottom of the stairs crying hysterically! I think she was more scared than hurt. Me too, scared that is.

This winter, we were getting the kids ready to go play in one of the first snows. We are snow people. We love it!!! I used to ski and Steve would play pond hockey. We know how to dress for hours of winter weather fun. We were starting to get the kids into their snow clothes, quite a daunting task. Remember that kid in the Christmas Story who couldn't put his arms down? We make him look underdressed. Sean must've gotten tired of waiting and ended up outside in just an undershirt, turtleneck, sweatpants and socks!! Even despite our best efforts of lockdown, the little bugger still manages to get out.

The day I wrote this was the most terrifying yet. Sean had unlocked the door and disappeared. I was frantic! I felt like I had lost my mind!! I knew he was gone but I didn't want to believe it. I checked everywhere in the house, I even looked in the closets, basement and the garage. Our neighbor friend was over playing at the time Sean disappeared. She was only 4 and she didn't understand what was happening. I tried to explain but I'm sure it didn't make sense. I told the girls in the house whose ages range from five, four and two to stay in the house. I ran barefoot up the block to see if Sean was at the cross street. He likes to watch the traffic go by sometimes. I ran past some kids in our neighborhood that knew Sean and asked them if they had seen him. All the kids said no. I told them to come get me if they found him. I then ran back home and called Steve. I had just spoken to him fifteen minutes earlier and said it was fine if he took a coworker out to dinner. Now when I spoke to Steve, I told him Sean was missing and I was calling 911 and our friend Sheila so he needed to get home ASAP. Meanwhile, I had gotten the attention of our neighbor. It may have been my screaming Sean's name over and over again, you think? (Even if Sean had heard me calling his name, he wouldn't answer). The neighbors were all preparing to search for him. I called my friend Sheila who arrived in what felt like seconds. Then I called 911. It has taken longer to type this than it happened in actual time. Sheila arrived while I was on the phone with the 911 operator, who was great but if she told me one more time to calm down, obscenities would've started flying out of my mouth! She asked how old he was, what he was wearing, and what he looked like. I don't know!!!! Didn't you hear me? I said my autistic son was MISSING!! He can't tell you his name or address. He can't be outside alone!! When Sheila arrived she knew I couldn't think clearly, so she thought for me. She said, " I would look behind the house." She found him in less than a minute. He had wandered behind my house and down to the creek. He was barefoot, in boxer shorts and a t-shirt. He was looking for "the creepy cave". Fortunately it wasn't too cold outside that day. Steve then arrived home to find Sean safe. At that point, he gave me a glass of wine to calm my nerves. Incidentally, the 911 operator never dispatched the police to our location or called back to follow up with this crisis. I have never been so scared in my whole life.

5. Mediator

One that mediates between parties at variance. (Dictionary Version)

SANDY: I am what some may consider a **Type A** person. That would be the most accurate way to describe my personality type. I'm a type A with a little mix of passive aggressive- aggressive mixed in. I'm like a personality mutt you might say. A **Type A** person who married another **Type A** person and procreated together. What do you think the outcome of that union would be? That's exactly what I thought. I am an outgoing, outspoken, talkative woman who gave birth to her twin, T.C. He has my personality reincarnate. Mike, on the other hand is also a TYPE **A** person. Well a **Type A** personality at his job, a **Type A minus** as a parent. He tends to be more laid back with the family. Ryan has a lot of his Dad's traits, thank God. He is a little more relaxed and can sit back and be introspective. The only problem is when you put a **Type A** boy, like T.C., who is outspoken and doesn't yet understand personal space with a **TYPE A minus,** non-verbal boy with autism, you get a drill sergeant that likes to push his brother's buttons. Again, autism not withstanding, all siblings do this. I just feel bad because T.C. feels this need to take care of his little brother and he can come across as either bossy or trying to be Ryan's parent. They are best friends at fifteen months apart, and no one lights up in a room like Ryan when he is playing with his big brother T.C. It's just that sometimes the boy with autism, who has a social disorder, and the outspoken "mayor," sometimes mix like oil and water. At times it can take a lot of mediating. I hear a lot of "I didn't do that" or "Ryan did it, not me!" The problem is, Ryan can't speak for himself, and so some mysteries go unsolved. Sometimes I try to be crafty and use the whole "I know what happened, because I have eyes in the back of my head" line, but T.C. is starting to figure that one out! So, here I am typing this book and I hear the pitter patter of little innocent feet upstairs. I hear a thump, and then I hear Ryan crying, so I yell up. What are you doing?? "Nothing" says T.C. "Then why is Ryan crying?" He's sad because Daddy's not home. Sure, nice try, I'm sure that's why he is crying, but I couldn't be more blessed with these

14

two boys. T.C. takes such good care of his brother and it's hard to resist asking for his help. Sometimes I'm not even aware of the pressure I put on him for such a young boy. T.C. was on vacation with his Aunt Sue so not only did he get one on one but also Mike and I spent quality time with just Ryan. With T.C. gone, I now realize how many things he does for his brother both voluntarily and not so voluntarily. That is the balancing acts all parents' with special needs children versus typical children walk. It is hard not to appear like you are playing favorites.

T.C. and Ryan Hallett at Christmas, 2008

NIKKI: Sean would say, "Are you are all right?" when he got hurt. I thought it was adorable until I learned what echolalia was. (When a person with autism uses repetitive speech and coined phrases) My daughter Caley, out of defense against Sean, who is twice her size, likes to bite and pinch him. She hits and screams and the only thing he does is ask, "Did you bite?" Although, she has learned to make a sound that absolutely drives him NUTS! It hurts his brain. He is then compelled to poke her in the eyes! What the heck? Where did that come from? He's never watched the three stooges. Yes, we freaked out the first time it happened (and every time after too).

When I think of mediating I think of the perpetual Dennis Leary's Rant that our life has become. "Where are your shoes? No you can't have cookies for breakfast! Get off the table! Give me those cookies! Who are you? Don't give the dog cookies! That's not your shoe it's your brother's. Put down those cookies!!" In our house, "Sean, stop fast-forwarding the DVD, no AB (repeat) button, Sean screams NO

ABC! Caley, don't hit your sister with the fishing pole! Kiera, where are your clothes? Sean, no AB button! (Sean screams again) NO ABC! Caley stop hitting Sean! Kiera don't eat your shoe!" This can go on for hours; they just don't give up— I do, out of shear exhaustion. All this is usually followed up by;" YOU (Sean), go upstairs and don't touch your poop. YOU (Caley), go in the kitchen, sit in a chair, and don't touch your poop. YOU (Kiera), go in the playroom and DON'T touch OR eat your poop! " What's the saying S—t happens!? Tell me about it.

6. Magicians

One who is an entertainer and is skilled in producing illusion by sleight of hand, deceptive devices, etc.; conjurer.
(Dictionary Version)

SANDY: *"ABRACADBRA."* Make the mess disappear. When you're in a hurry and you need the illusion that you are an organized and clean mother of the year, what do you do? Pull an illusion out of somewhere. I love the definition. The words deception, disappearing, and illusion can be so descriptive. Hmmm, I could probably think of a few other examples. Say we're having company and they will be arriving in a short amount of time. I can usually clean up pretty quick because I try not to let the mess get too out of hand. Just don't give a tour of the closets, cupboards or the basement to your guests. Some things you can hide in inconspicuous places but eventually you have to clean them out. I am a culprit of putting everything in cupboards. I hid things in the bathroom cupboards and the kitchen cupboards. My first clue would be when I can't close the cupboard doors. So, what do I do? I shove the debris in the cupboard and slam the door shut. Eventually I will need to re-open the cupboards. What am I, ten? I know it's just a quick fix for later, but what can I say. Hide stuff under the bed too? That's what I say. I'm not sure why I feel the need to give off the illusion of a perfect clean house when guests come over. (Maybe if my home is clean and organized, the illusion is- all aspects of my life are clean and organized to the bystander. Those closest to me can probably see through my smoke screen.) They know I have two kids under the age of seven. I suppose one of the reasons may be I need to feel I have a little control in my life. A clean house, though only clean occasionally will show people I appear to have some control over what happens in my home. What a crazy illusion!

NIKKI: *"Kiera, don't eat that crayon!"* POOF! *Just like magic it disappears!!!* *"Sean, you can't eat that entire bag of Doritos!"* POOF! *Gone! Out of sight- out of mind! Caley you can't wear your pajamas to school again."* Lately Kiera has been *quite the little Houdini. Somehow she has managed to get out of her straight jacket. (Not literally of course!) I made her clothes a little harder to get out of. You see she likes to strip and unfortunately she is a poop investigator too. So I put her "onsies" on the outside of her leggings. But somehow, magically, she has started getting the leggings off while still wearing the "onesie", still snapped and everything. Pretty impressive for a beginner!*

Seriously, I'd say I'm more of an illusionist. I can give the illusion I'm calm and peaceful and in control most of the time. I was trained at a young age to smile when you answer the phone. No matter what is going on in the background I'm happy you called. The ladies at all the therapy offices always say, "How is it you are always smiling?" Fake it till you make it I say. If I believe we will be ok we will be ok. Sometimes in the heat of the moment I lose my way, but usually I can bring it back.

7. Clown/Comedian

One who is a fool, jester, in entertainment. (Dictionary Version)

SANDY: As you may be able to tell already I love to joke and laugh! I know who doesn't love to laugh? I may burn more calories laughing than I do swimming or chasing my kids. Part of that is my warped sense of humor. My sense of humor is warped or dry, with a dash of sophomoric humor. Part of my key to raising a child with special needs is to add levity to crazy situations. Mike and I can be pretty goofy people. We make a lot of funny voices and sound effects. I also sing A LOT. Understand I have one of the deepest, off key voices for a woman I know. How many times do telemarketers call and they refer to the lady of the house as SIR? At our house this phenomenon happens a lot. When Ryan and I have to go to a doctor's appointment, we get through it by me singing the goofiest songs to him. The more hand gestures I add the better the song is to him. You still can't go wrong with the Alphabet song or The Itsy Bitsy Spider song. Mike and I both like to jive them up with original extended dance versions, adding extra moves or our own version of the original lyrics. Nothing makes me happier than watching Ryan's face light up or hearing that deep belly laugh when you sing to him or tickle him. Knock knock jokes are still cool for T.C. He's a funny kid! He also has a great sense of humor. T.C. loves to make Ryan laugh with funny faces and tickles. He is also one of those physical comics who fall down a lot for laughs like Kramer on Seinfeld. We do enjoy a little tickle torture all around, too. At dinner, T.C. always has to go to the bathroom in the middle of the meal. I tell him everyday to wait until we're finished, but he still has to go right then! He'll be standing there, jumping up and down, and holding himself with all of the drama he can muster. Finally, one night at dinnertime, Ryan, T.C. and I were eating at the table when he asked if he could go to the bathroom. I gave him the same song and dance I gave him every night but in the end, I conceded. He went into the bathroom, but he was taking FOREVER. (Like the "Sandlot" Forever! for all of you movie buffs.) I asked him, "What is taking you so long?" His witty retort at age six year was "Mom, cant' you just let me Live My Life?" And then he giggled. This . . .is coming from the mouth of babes. My witty retort was "you're killing me Small's." (Another "Sandlot classic!!!)

NIKKI: We'll do anything for a laugh! For my son's sixth birthday, I brought cupcakes to school. I was very dressed up, like wedding reception dress attire, yet I wore a felt birthday cake hat with candles on it. My husband said, "You have brass ones."
   Are their any "Oliver" fans? I'd do anything for a smile, anything! My husband Steve is kid number four. . Krusty the Clown, from the "Simpsons." In fact one of the reasons I married him is because of how funny he is and how great he is with kids. When we go swimming he loves to throw the kids in the pool and scream, "I'll give you a raise!!!" (From "The Great Muppet Caper") He has this great talent of drawing the attention to himself and away from the kids. He doesn't care how silly or goofy he is as long as it makes the kids laugh. They love it too. He does silly voices too, which can always bring a smile. He imitates Grover, Elmo, Bob the builder, and many other favorites.
   I don't get to play with the kids as much as I'd like, so they are really impressed when I get dressed up like Winnie the Pooh for Halloween (I have a whole body costume, I could do birthday parties). No one can ever say I lack commitment or dedication. There is no mask, just my face, but still, the first few times the kids see me in it, they seemed a little freaked out since it appeared the bear ate Mommy and that's how she got in that suit! I've been Winnie the Pooh for I think the last seven or eight years now. The neighbors are always impressed at my dedication, especially the Halloween it was eighty degrees outside.

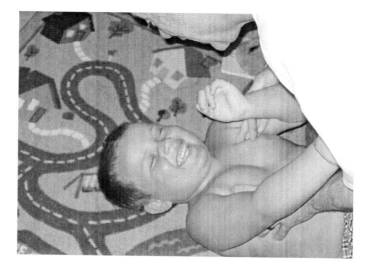

Steve Wisor making Ryan Hallett laugh hysterically, 2008

8. Plumber

Assemble, install, and repair pipes, fittings, and fixtures of heating, water, and drainage systems, according to specifications and plumbing codes. (Dictionary Version)

SANDY: I would like to think of myself as a pseudo plumber. Not because I have occasionally shown "crack" in my low-rise jeans. It's because, as I have previously explained, my husband isn't home a lot so I have to do some home projects. I may at times become a little too over excited and I bite off a little more than I can chew. Our toilet was continuously running and I was about to commit myself to an asylum. Instead of calling a plumber at eight thousand dollars a minute, I decided to empower myself to take a trip to Home Depot and search for the parts of the toilet by myself. I, with my kids in tow in the store, found most of the parts all by myself. I am WOMAN- hear me roar! I bought the bobber doohickey and I switched it out in two toilets. I admit it, I fixed them, but they weren't perfect. My neighbor Jamie- Mr. Fixit, and Mike finally corrected the teeny, weenie errors that may have occurred. Wouldn't you know that darn toilet still sticks a little sometimes? I didn't say I was great at "fix it" projects, did I? Besides fixing toilets I am a heck of a *plunger*. Not plumber, but *plunger*. We have to have one next to every toilet. As you know children like to watch things twirl down the toilet in that quick, circular motion. Ryan on the other hand, not only likes to put foreign objects in the toilets, but he likes to wash his hands in the toilet and put his hands in his mouth. Gross, how nasty is that! Can you say E-coli? I wonder if Ryan will ever learn that sticking his hands in the toilet or eating off of the floor of the bathroom is extremely unsanitary! I can only clean so much, right?

NIKKI: Sean went up to the master bathroom, plugged the sink with the stopper and turned the water on. He was armed with a high-powered rechargeable battery operated lantern. He loves to play in standing water. He locked the door and played. (Out of the range of the baby monitor) You know when it has been TOO long and

TOO quiet, it is time to investigate. I went upstairs and followed the sound of running water. I unlocked the door to find him in the dark, with the lantern, in the water. (Again, his guardian angel is working overtime.) Water was flowing, over the sink, down the cupboards, covering the floor and down into the heating ducts. I removed him from the Master bath and proceeded to clean up in "complete panic mode". I was so engrossed in cleaning up the mess I didn't notice that Sean has moved on to yet ANOTHER bathroom. He closes that drain, turns on that water, and locks the door and leaves to go into his bedroom. Steve then calls to tell me he is coming home from work. I tell him the story of how Sean has flooded the master bath, and I need him to come upstairs as soon as he gets home. I am in the process of cleaning the bathroom and running to get more towels to sop up the mess in the water hazard, formerly our bathroom, when I heard the water running in the kid's bathroom. About that time Steve gets home and tries to use his Beer making kit (received as a Christmas gift) to siphon the water out of the HVAC system in the master bath while I went to investigate the kids bathroom. The water was just starting to overflow by the time I got the door unlocked. In the aftermath of the chaos, Steve's brilliance rang through. He grabbed a lot of the available Good Nights diapers and he proceeded to clean up the mess of water the siphon wouldn't get. It only took a whole pack (at seventeen dollars a pop.)

9. Maid

A woman or girl employed to do domestic work.
(Dictionary Version)

SANDY: Ryan has another hobby he enjoys. His artistic side, he inherited from yours truly, shines through when he gets into the master bath and finds the toothpaste. His rendition of Van Gogh's "Starry Night" is pretty accurate. My mother warned me when I was growing up how toothpaste can stain and takes the color out of everything. Well, guess what? Dear old Mom was right. One day Ryan snuck into our master bath and found the Scooby-Doo toothpaste. Between sucking on the end because it tastes like bubblegum, and the squirting of the toothpaste on the bed, we had quite a mess! It was on his hands, his mouth, my comforter, the floor and then the trail led to his bedroom before we caught him! Three bed comforters later, some steam cleaning and a few odds and ends in the garbage, most of the toothpaste trail was finally gone. That is until next time. We keep those doorknob locks on the bathroom but he must sense when we forget to close the door.

I don't know if any of you have a child with texture issues but my son Ryan has major issues! When he eats food, he will only trust the taste if he likes the feel of it in his hands. All foods are crumpled and smashed as he eats them. He cannot use utensils, or possibly just chooses not too. If given the choice he would probably opt for the latter. He will only eat crunchy texture foods to slightly chewy. Runny, cold, or mushy is out of the question. You can imagine mealtime at our house. He only uses his hands and a majority of the food ends up on the floor under the kitchen table. Of course on spaghetti night he usually escapes the confines of the kitchen and runs into the living room (beige, earth tones) and jumps hand first onto the couch. Sometimes he may even venture upstairs if my back is turned. It is like the fairy tale of Hansel and Gretel. I follow the crumb trail until I find him. Of course you have his "non spill" sippy cup he still uses because he cannot drink out of a cup. Red drinks are taboo in our home. I know "red dye number forty" and our builder grade, cream, wall-to-wall carpeting don't agree with each other. Ryan will only drink a full sippy cup, which he continually shakes up and down to test the volume of liquid. This is when millions of tiny droplets of juice embed themselves in our carpeting everywhere! Guess what I asked for on our eleven-year wedding anniversary. You guessed it! It was a steam cleaner for our carpet. I've already been through two of them. Vacuums are our best friends, too! In all seriousness, it can be very confusing and frustrating chasing your child all over the house and finding one mess after the other. That is the same for all kids; the degree of the mess may be a little more out of control. My friends and I just try to keep each other on an email chain for the best cleaning remedies. We use Oxy clean for carpeting and magic eraser for walls. You understand where I am coming from. We can't be in all places all of the times.

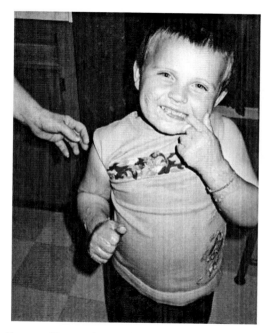

Ryan Eating Peanut Butter in our kitchen and sharing it with everyone, 2006

NIKKI: A maid doesn't begin to define what we do. I tell people my maid quit years ago and is in witness relocation. A bit of advice, if you get a diagnosis of Autism Spectrum Disorder in your family- put in linoleum or hardwood wherever you can. We have slip covered every piece of furniture in our home! Make your home one hundred percent washable! It's just easier. Not everything fits in the washing machine. If it's NOT washable, don't buy it. Trust me, you'll thank me later. Linoleum is handy in our kitchen. I own a mop, but I can't say I actually mop the kitchen floor. When Kiera spills the dog water on the floor, I take a kitchen towel and mop the floor with it. I put washcloths under each foot and "skate" around the kitchen. I wash windows daily, too. This is due to the markers, yogurt, cool whip and other various substances that accumulate on the sliding glass door and sixty-two inch bay window in the kitchen. Thank God for the dog, otherwise I would be vacuuming food and crumbs, everyday, ALL DAY.

When Sean gets stomach bugs, sees food he doesn't like or basically feels like puking, he can't do it in a toilet, sink or any container for that matter. I used to use a bath towel to sop it up. I would drape myself in the towel, hug him and hope the puke hits the towel. I've moved from bath towels to kitchen towels. They are smaller, a little less gross and easier to wash. If Sean gets sick in the middle of the night and we can't get to him in time, our first concern is with Sean, not the mess. We can always clean the mess later. We usually lock the carnage on the towels in the tub, in the kid's bathroom, and get to it later. It never fails, it happens the night before a trip, or during one! Caley runs away when she has to throw up. Luckily she doesn't get as many stomach bugs as Sean. It is less frequent for her to puke, but she runs away like she is trying to get away from it. Who knows where it will end up? Thank God Kiera hasn't gotten sick yet (knock on wood). But I'm sure she'll manage her own way of doing things, like everyone else.

10. Athletic Coach/Personal Trainer

A person who is trained or skilled in exercises, sports, or games requiring physical strength, agility, or stamina.
(Dictionary Version)

SANDY: In our family we have two coaches. I grew up as a swimmer and later became a swim coach. I had the privilege to coach swimming at a small Division III college in Alliance, Ohio called Mount Union. That is my husband's alma mater. I had the good fortune of being the assistant of an amazing woman, Kathie Lavery. She used to bring her two little girls to practice with her every day and I saw how much they enjoyed swimming at that age. We still get back to Alliance in the summers to visit our friends the Mastroianni's. Kathie runs the pool they belong to so when we visit we have a great time showing Kathie the progress the boys have made from the previous summer. I would like to take the credit of saying I used my lifeguarding and coaching skills to help teach my kids to swim, but that would only be a small part of it. Ryan has the body of a football player but the love of water like a swimmer. Since he was a baby he could naturally hold his breath and blow the bubbles out. He propels himself in a non-traditional manner but it gets the job done. We went swimming the other day and he swam the whole length of the pool (twenty yards) and then some. If we were in the deep end of a pool he would continue to swim without stopping. It is the most amazing thing you've ever witnessed. The reason I say deep end is because he enjoys bouncing off of the bottom of the pool. If he can touch he will cheat and only bob up and down. Two years ago we took him to the Cincinnati Zoo and the manatee mesmerized him. He had never shown any interest in animals before. He stood in front of the aquarium like they were old friends. He would run along the front of the aquarium and chase it to keep up. When he gets in the pool sometimes, he crosses his legs and rolls under water. He morphs and rolls like nothing I can explain. Maybe he was a manatee in a prior life.

My husband is also a coach. He was the head football coach for another small Division III college in Northern Kentucky named Thomas More

College. He just recently took the head football-coaching job at another Division III school, Heidelberg University in Tiffin, Ohio. When we began this book we were planning on moving to be with him after we sold our house. Now, I live in Tiffin with him and our kids. (I digress) Needless to say, we are big, loud, energetic, motivated people, who can either be beneficial for kids or not, depending on whom you ask. I would like to think our energy level is what keeps us going. One of the hardest things about being a coach is to speculate if your child will ever play a competitive sport. Not that it is that important. If they want to, great, if not, that is OK, too. It is just wondering if the future will allow us to make that choice or if the disability will make it for us. We worked with Ryan a lot to see if he would throw balls or catch them. As I said earlier, toys may be played with inappropriately or not understood by some children with autism. Ryan showed no interest in balls for a long time. He slowly understands the concept of a ball and he may catch one or throw one. The irony of that is on picture day at his school this year, the photographer handed him a football as a prop and what did he do with it? He threw it! First time ever and it was supposed to be used as a prop! Now we attend all of the football games as a family with our MP3 players, portable DVD players and plenty of snacks. It's not so bad!

NIKKI: Personal Trainer, who needs one? When was the last time you spent 15 minutes jumping on a trampoline with three kids? Try it! You'll like it. Bouncing is so much more fun than a treadmill, just ask Tigger. Going to any store is always an adventure. Where's my Indiana Jones hat? I have to go to Wal-mart. (Where's my hat? I want to wear my hat!) Did I mention chasing a two year old, a four year old and a seven year old around a Wal-Mart Super Center or a Payless shoe store? Let's just say the mall is an aerobic exercise. Walking around the block as a family is a HUGE feat too! "Sean, get back here! Caley don't pick the neighbors flowers! Kiera, don't eat the neighbors rocks!" Also, chasing naked children around is pretty aerobic too. They always seem to head for the stairs. And pee while you're chasing them.

Our most recent public nakedness was at the playground when Dad decided to bring water pistols and fill them in the water fountain. You see one of Sean's sensory issues is he cannot keep wet clothes on his body. It doesn't matter where he is he takes his clothes off. Can't tell you how many times he tries to get naked at the pool when he's done swimming and ready to go home.

11. Travel Agent

A person engaged in selling and arranging transportation, accommodations, tours, or trips for travelers. (Dictionary Version)

SANDY: Traveling with any children can be a nightmare. My kids are fortunately pretty good when it comes to traveling. Our friends, the Mastroianni's, piled their three kids into an RV to drive down and see one of my husband's football games. Needless to say, they haven't been back. Jenny told me stories of how her kids would scream and run around in the RV the whole way down. She said that's pretty typical for most kids. Recently we were taking a trip. Mike was driving, I was co-pilot and Ryan and T.C. were in the backseat with their portable DVD player. It's a great invention, but if it's on his lap Ryan will hit the reset button every chance he gets. So, we're driving along and I hear the introduction to the movie about twenty times. Before I was conscious of what was happening I turned around and saw T.C. was sleeping so Ryan had total control of the DVD player. We had to take it away before he broke it. With no distractions, Ryan learned how to get halfway out of his booster seat. He figured out he could put the shoulder strap behind him and lean forward. That was a nightmare! He was already mad because we took away the DVD player. He pulled down the seat belt, leaned forward and grabbed the seat in front of him where I was seated. He grabbed a huge chunk of my hair and pulled it hard! Yikes, that hurt! His car seat is no longer seated behind the driver's seat any more.

This year our family vacation was in Sandusky, Ohio, My sister-in-law Sue owns property on Lake Erie. The kids love it there but it is a five-hour drive from Kentucky. While we are there we like to swim and go boating on Uncle Rick's boat. The property is located near Cedar Point, the amusement park. On the Fourth of July we took our first trip to Cedar Point with the boys. The problem with an amusement park is it is great for Ryan because he seeks the thrill rides for speed and spinning but the down side is someone has to ride with him on the rides. *That would be me.* The rides are worth it. He gets the vestibular motion he seeks and you get to see his face grinning from ear to ear. I, of course, want to puke on all of those circular rides. How do you explain the laws of patience to a non-verbal child with autism, waiting in lines for rides? I got pinched A LOT that night. Mike's sister had talked about us all eventually going to Disney World together. They would love that! I hear "the greatest place on earth" is very disability friendly. Someone told me if you call ahead they can make some allowances for children with special needs, which may include avoiding long lines. The lines, the noise, the heat, Yikes! We'll go someday, but I'm not ready for the planes, trains and automobiles trip to Florida just yet.

T.C. and Ryan at the Newport Aquarium in Newport, Kentucky, 2007

NIKKI: Bud is always amazed at the amount of stuff I need to bring everywhere! What can I say? I like to be prepared! Currently I am making a list for a trip to the ENT (ear, nose and throat doctor). I will need pull-ups for Sean and Caley, diapers and wipes for Kiera, and a change of clothes for all three of them. As I mentioned earlier, Sean will get naked if his clothes get wet no matter where he is. So I have to be prepared for rain getting his clothes wet, a malfunction in a water fountain, or a rogue water balloon. You see there is just no reasoning with him. Maybe it's the autism or obsessive-compulsive disorder, but it's impossible! Also I'll need the portable DVD player accompanied with DVD's. Two "video now juniors" (a handheld DVD player for small kids), stroller, double stroller, drinks, two water bottles, a sippy cup, snacks, books, color magic markers and paper. Sean will carry his backpack and help push the stroller. (You see we use the backpack to provide deep pressure input and maybe stop him from running away from me) I thought about bringing a game boy, CD player and Walkman for Sean and Caley. Remember this is only for a forty-five minute appointment. Can you imagine what I bring for a twelve-hour car trip when we visit our family in Pennsylvania! By the way, we got to the appointment and the ear-nose-throat doctor's office was playing "Finding Nemo" on the TV. **Game, Set, Match.** *Nothing more was needed. Like I always say better to be prepared than unprepared.*

In the future I would strongly suggest if you are driving more than three hours always bring a large supply of Ziploc bags, trash bags, a roll of paper towels, baby wipes and Clorox wipes. (I'll get back to the reason why later) I will never get caught off guard again!! It's also wise to travel with outlet covers and cabinet locks. You never know when a house is unprepared for small children. Also, we bring putty for hanging posters and to put up alert alarms on doors and windows so it won't cause any permanent damage. Suction cups for windows are also a must have. You don't want the kids to escape or fall out of windows. Never underestimate a child with autism. They are so covert they could work for the CIA. They're crafty and skillful at escaping. They could star in the movie "Mission Impossible!"

12. Dietician/Food Police

One who has the science or art of applying the principles of nutrition to the diet or one who monitors the variety of food eaten, amount of food snuck from the cupboards or the amount of food consumed. (Dictionary Version and Our Version)

SANDY: I admit Ryan's diet is less than fantastic. I serve dinner on cafeteria trays to remind myself to serve both kids foods from four basic food groups. Unless of course it is pizza, that covers them all! We have always supplemented Ryan with vitamins and supplements to balance his diet as best as we could. Where do I begin? How do you supplement someone's diet when they don't eat anything too cold, too hot, too green, or too mushy? Most children with special needs are very picky eaters. We had something called an IGG and IGE allergy test for Ryan via his physician. It was administered and sent through Great Plains laboratory with Dr. William Shaw. Ryan has sensitivities with the protein casein. It was off the chart. What that basically means is Ryan has sensitivities to milk products and if he eats or drinks them it could make him sick. He has a slight sensitivity to the protein gluten. That is the protein you find in all breads. We did the gluten, casein free diet for over a year. I now know how Ryan reacts to certain foods so now we modify his diet. He has a large appetite, but he only eats meats, breads and potatoes. He may occasionally eat a couple of vegetables and no fruits, unless they are dried, or of course a fruit snack. Unfortunately that doesn't really count! Fortunately he hates ice cream and condiments. These are a few of my vices. Not to mention they are really messy if he did eat them! If fruit snacks, french fries and chicken nuggets didn't exist my son would be skin and bones. There is a lot of trial and error with foods we serve him. I once read somewhere you have to serve the same thing twelve times before they may try the food once. Ergo, we waste a lot of food! I would continuously put a small bowl of applesauce in front of him. I try it with dinner all of the time. How could he not like applesauce! Everyone likes applesauce. Applesauce is even popular in pop culture; to quote Peter Brady from the "Brady Bunch",

"*Pork Chops and applesauce, sound swell*". I served him the applesauce. He touched it and I watched him physically gag! I did it eleven more times because I believe EVERYTHING I read. I am SO kidding! I'll bet you never knew the diet could be so hard for kids with autism did you? The problem is not necessarily the taste, but the texture. I hope my son doesn't grow up obese because of his diet. Because of his genetics he is already an eighty-two pound, six year old and I can barely pick him up. I worry about how big and strong he will be in just a few years.

Ryan eating birthday cake at the Lake Erie Condo in the summer of 2007. We offered him the fork he just chooses not to use it!

NIKKI: My kids all have unique eating habits. Don't get me started with Kiera. Like I mentioned before she eats everything. Sean could eat nothing but Powdered donuts= "GFC" (gold fish color) and Pretzel rods= "P". We have to speak in special code because Sean can spell out words. Sean will eat anything brown and crunchy. For example, he likes chocolate peanut butter cups and pretzels. My three kids all have unique eating habits. Sean could live on pretzels and chocolate alone but never a chocolate covered pretzel! If it has sugar in it, count Caley in. As for Kiera, we have to stop her from eating EVERYTHING. Literally.

Things Kiera will eat:
Mud and Sand   **VS.**

Things Kiera won't eat:
Oatmeal

Grass and mulch	*VS.*	*Pudding*
Shoes and make-up	*VS.*	*Jello jigglers*
Wooden tables and chairs	*VS.*	*Bread crumbs*
Dressers	*VS.*	*Craisins*
Toothbrushes	*VS.*	*Clementine oranges*
DVD players	*VS.*	*Jello*

. . . And most recently a glass Christmas ornament.

Kiera is not just experimenting with chewing pencils with erasers, markers, crayons, books and rocks, but she is actually ingesting them!! I can't believe she doesn't weigh three hundred pounds. I feed her when I catch her eating something inappropriate. It is probably from my Italian upbringing. EAT, EAT!!! When she eats a pencil I give her fruit snacks. If she's eating the rubber backing on carpeting, I give her a pretzel rod. Caley seems to prefer more dairy products. She loves milk, yogurt, macaroni and cheese, ice cream and any version of cheese, grated or sliced. She'll eat chicken nuggets, tacos and pizza, but rarely will she try a hot dog or hamburger. She could survive living on a stranded island by just eating peanut butter and jelly sandwiches. She is also a junk food addict! Favorites include potato chips especially Pringles, cheese curls and Doritos. Caley also enjoys raw pizza dough, pancake batter and cookie dough. Salmonella anyone??? Her four basic food groups do NOT include vegetables of any kind. Not unless you can count pizza sauce as one. When are WE going to acknowledge pizza as the perfect food? The closest food to a vegetable Caley will eat is a French fry. I know it's a starch, but I'm desperate. I have a recipe I haven't tried yet but it includes spinach in brownies. Are their any takers out there? Sandy's reaction was barf! The only green thing Caley has ever eaten is the turtle in her "Finding Nemo" fruit snacks. I've tried hiding veggies like carrots in spaghetti sauce but unless it's cooked or pureed like baby food she'll pick it out. Never put anything in pizza either. It can be too messy. Her most recent phrase when she was referring to a pizza from a new place (with visible spices) was "EEEWWW, that's disgusting, I won't eat that!!!" Nice, huh?

There were fruits that Sean used to eat such as blueberries, apples, raisins and grapes. He also used to eat vegetables like broccoli, potatoes, peas, carrots, vegetable soup, and salad. Other foods would be barbeque ribs, and Chinese food. This has been his only area of regression. I'm sure the average person would not remember the "Blue's clues applesauce". Yes, it was blue, obviously artificially colored, but it was berry flavored. When I couldn't find it on the shelf, I discovered it was discontinued. I went into a PANIC! I emailed Motts and everyone in my address book to see if they could find some. My well-meaning friend's and family suggested we just add food coloring to the applesauce. WHY DON'T THEY UNDERSTAND IT'S NOT THE SAME? It has a different flavor, different color and a different taste. I found a wholesale dealer on line that sold me a case for $90.00. It never arrived! I was more *upset about not getting the applesauce than I was about not getting the money back...which I did get a refund about a month later. I was devastated. Mott's did come out with a mixed berry pink version of the applesauce. Since then, he will eat it occasionally. It was so important because it was the only fruit left in his diet. Surely he'd get scurvy or something from no fruit in his diet. He also eliminated juice boxes because his well meaning Mother put medicine in it and it fermented. He used to eat Dole's frozen fruit bars, but one slight change in color, packaging or texture. "Forget about it". He refused to eat it. Talk about frustrating!*

*Sean and Caley have their issues but as for Kiera. Just when you thought it was safe to go in to the other room . . . **Dum Dum Dum**- Jaws eats Eyore (the tailless donkey in Winnie the Pooh) off of the wall!*

Kiera Wisor eating pizza and drinking juice in her kitchen in 2007

13. Electrician

One, who installs, maintains, operates, or repairs electrical equipment. (Dictionary Version)

SANDY: Like all homes with smaller children, you have to safeguard your home from electrical mishaps. We have the basic outlet covers. We have had some problems with objects finding their way down the heating ducts so we are careful to keep most of the grates closed. Our family is big into appliances. We buy a lot of TV's, VCR's and DVD players. Let me rephrase that. We replace a lot of TV's, VCR's and DVD players! When you get children with autism there can be an issue of repetition. Ryan plays with the buttons on the TV until they fall off. He ejects the VCR tape until it gets wound up in the gears. He likes to watch the disc open and shut repeatedly until the motor runs out. We have lost or worn out more remotes than I can keep count of. T.C. got a couple of those new TV games you plug into the front of the TV. It has a joystick with it. We had Sponge Bob and Ms. Pac Man. Those lasted a couple months before Ryan chewed through the cords. It's scary! The mouse on our computer needs replaced because of the chord. He doesn't understand the chord is electric. He only understands the sensory feeling he craves so he puts everything in his mouth! We were visiting our friends, the Hartman's. All of the adults were sitting in the family room watching a movie and we all smelled something burning. Ryan had burrowed himself in the corner, behind the TV and was biting a hole in the chord of the portable DVD player we had brought with us. We were all surprised he wasn't shocked or that there house didn't burn down. Either way we were very lucky Ryan didn't get hurt.

NIKKI: Sean sprayed Windex cleaner on the computer monitor, so it fried one of the computer's. He had colored on it with crayons and he was trying to clean it. How can you get mad about that? We still don't know who put the penny in the car lighter, either. It shorted the fuse in the car. It was major! We have also extracted CD's from the VCR. Sean likes to watch things over and over again. Unfortunately the girls don't. Fast Forward is his favorite button on the VCR's and the AB repeat button on the DVD player is his favorite, too. He burns grooves in the DVD's so they skip. I am told it is one of his self-stimulating behaviors called stemming. Whatever it's called, it drives the rest of us crazy. Buy cheap electronics and replace often imagine the money I could've saved if I actually knew what I was doing!

List of appliances we have been through:

7 VCR's in 7 years.   *3 boom boxes*
4 walkmans   *3 portable CD players'*
4 camera's (2 digital),   *3 computers*
3 vacuums   *2 cordless phones*
2 TV VCR's for cars   *2 portable DVD players*
2 PlayStation 2's,   *countless controllers*
5 Baby monitors   *7 computer mouse's.*

14. Weight Lifter

One who lifts barbells or weights as an exercise. (Dictionary Version)

SANDY: Back in the day I was an athlete. I have finally gotten back into exercising again. I use it as an outlet for stress. Actually I exercise for the stress as well as the addiction to endorphins! It has taken a long time for me to spend time on myself away from my kids free of guilt. (I'm Catholic) That was part of the reason. The other reason was because it was time to lose some baby weight six years after Ryan was born. When the kids and I go to the YMCA I work out for a half hour and then we play together in the pool. I swim and walk on the treadmill or the elliptical. I lift weights at home since I needed to build strength. When my husband is on the road for football games someone has to carry those beautiful boys to bed. They each weigh about eighty-five pounds! When they were born Ryan was ten pounds, four ounces at thirty-eight weeks and T.C. was nine pounds, two ounces full term. I won't be able to pick them up forever, but when the kids wake up with a bad dream or they are sick I want to be able to hold them while they are still young. One of my favorite parts of the day is school time. I get off the bus from work and drive to Ryan's school and pick him up. He goes to a special school named Redwood. I adore all of his teachers. They have taught me a lot and they keep me posted daily on how well he is doing in school. When I get to Redwood, I meet him at the door of his classroom. He puts on his shoes, jacket and his backpack. I then give him a piggyback ride out to our car. I think he looks forward to it every day. It's our special time for me to hold him and sing the ABC's to him. Hopefully I can continue this tradition for a couple of more years. I guess I better start squatting heavier weights! After picking up Ryan, we drive home, wait for T.C. to get off the bus in front of our house and the three of us get to hang out together!

Sandy and Ryan at Goodridge Elementary at T.C. and Sean's recital, 2007

NIKKI: Why are our kids so heavy? In March of 2006 I had a hernia repaired. There were actually three of them. A seventy pound six year old can do that. Sean has always been above the ninety- ninth percentile. He was born at ten pounds, nine and a half ounces. Caley is only forty-five pounds at four years old. Kiera is thirty pounds at age two. The girl's weights are pretty average, but of course the heaviest needs to be held, lifted, and cuddled the most. We have daily piggyback rides from the bus to the house. Piggyback is the easiest, but not always the most convenient, especially when he jumps from the bottom step of the school bus into my arms. Caley is still forty-five pounds, but that is still manageable. Since I never go to the gym I made my own weights. I filled downy bottles, and tide bottles with water so they would be different weights. I do two loads of laundry a day, so I do eight repetitions of the bottles for my weight lifting. I do curls, triceps and military lifting. It is "quite a load". Get it? Laundry detergent!! Hee Hee.

15. Artist

One skilled or versed in learned arts. (Dictionary Version)

SANDY: I am a Kent State University graduate with a major in Art History and a duel minor in glass blowing and fiber arts and surface design. Needless to say, I have a bit of art in my blood. I loved to draw as a child and my oldest son T.C. carries around a sketchbook some of the time. Fortunately he got both sides of the brain where I only have the creative hemisphere. I try to encourage both kids to do art projects. We draw on paper and chalkboards and color in books. Ryan only scribbles but his scribbling has improved. The difficult thing with Ryan is he likes to chew on the crayons or markers. He is very oral. At school when he does a project for art they give him a chewy tube or a sucker to suck on so he doesn't ingest all of the writing utensils. Play-doh is another fun project. I can't stand the smell! Ryan loves to knead the play-doh, but again he may sneak some into his mouth, so we have to beware. We sometimes just play with shaving cream or finger paints. I'm not too brave in my house so those are basement or outdoor projects. One of my favorite projects with Ryan and T.C. was when were sitting in the basement with a huge bucket of play-doh. He was making some cool sculptures. I think the even cooler thing was he sat for longer than three minutes doing one project and he didn't ingest his whole masterpiece!!! They have come a long way with that stuff since I was a kid! It always makes me proud and amazed at the progression of art projects from just a few short years ago. I don't know if Ryan will have a big connection to art or music but whichever I am going along for the ride!

NIKKI: I have always enjoyed art. When I was a child, my parents would take me to the Philadelphia Art Museum every Sunday after church. It was free on Sundays until noon. My Mom made sure I learned about art to be cultured. My father wanted me to appreciate art because it runs in our blood. He worked in reinforced steel for forty years and would make these unique modern sculptures. He brought one of his sculptures home and my Mom said, "I give up what is it?" So that's what he named that piece. He sees art in everything and I like to think I've learned that from him. I took art lessons every Saturday for years. There was painting, drawing, sketching, sculpture, ceramics, and even photography. In high school, I was voted most creative. I took art for an elective every year I could. My teacher actually asked to keep one of my pieces, a paper-mache' bunny, that I didn't think was very good. Art like beauty is in the eye of the beholder. I took art classes on a scholarship on Saturdays at More College of Art in Philadelphia all through high school. I spent all day Saturday's creating art. I loved it so much! Saw my first naked male form at fifteen in one of my sketch classes. I was so embarrassed I couldn't draw anything near him. I think I ended up drawing the palm tree or plant behind him. I always thought I would be and artist. Actually I am because I made such beautiful children. But anyway, I was told I could never make any money or a career out of I so I settled for going to college for Elementary Education and perhaps I could be an art teacher someday.

Now in our home we have every kind of art supplies you can think of: markers, crayons, paints, chalk, clay, but the kid's favorite is to use washable markers. I like to express myself in art and I think my kids do too. We also like to color on the windows with window markers. Our basement is unfinished for the time being. The walls and floors in our basement are concrete and cinder block. We also use chalk on the floors and walls to play Blue's Clues. None of this is strange to me because when I was a kid my father once painted a scene on our basement walls. Then for my thirteenth birthday party he let me and my friends write our names and color all over the other walls. We had so much fun! I'll never forget it!

Sean is also very creative. He drew a circle at his one-year check-up. It totally freaked out the doctor. He asked what else Sean could draw. It was pretty funny. He also made a poop sculpture once. He pooped on the carpet in his room and stuck Geotrax pieces in it. I took a picture of it to show my husband. He was away in Australia. Sean started painting when he was about ten months old. When he was two, he water color painted a wiener dog, eating a carrot. That's Steve's take on it, but I still don't see it. He also likes to draw on the computer. He is very good at it. We think he learned how to draw from Blue's Clues when the old host, Steve, was on the show. Steve would draw step by step and that's how Sean's brain would remember it. He could draw a chair, bed and bricks, perfectly and exactly the way Steve did. He was three years old at the time.

Kiera enjoys drawing on all surfaces with anything she can get her hands on! That would include chalk, crayons, markers, pencils, poop, and certain toys. She also has an Elmo (fuzzy monster from Sesame Street) character with a crayon and a Wendy doll (from "Bob the Builder" cartoon) with a paintbrush, which together they color on the walls. Pretty tricky. She also eats erasers. Caley loves to paint, especially pumpkins and pictures of her Dad. Last summer Sean saw a tattooed man and asked Steve if he could paint him (Steve). All three kids painted over him. It was so much fun! The kids also enjoy Play-doh more than most kids. It gives them great sensory input. I'm thrilled my kids enjoy art so much. It feels like that part of me comes through them.

Sean Wisor painting a picture at home in 2005

16. Proctor and Gamble Stockholder

An extreme user and purchaser of highly taxable paper products. (Our Version)

SANDY: Whenever my family and I take a road trip up to Columbus or Cleveland we take Interstate Seventy-One. It is always cool driving back into Cincinnati to see the twin Proctor and Gamble buildings. When you see them you know you are almost home. I guess we take that local company to heart because we use so many of their products we should have bought stock when the kids were born. Its not that we use any different products than anyone else, it's just the sheer volume that would surprise someone!

*APPROXIMATE YEARLY DOLLAR VALUE FOR EACH PRODUCT (Both households combined)

-BOUNTY PAPER TOWELS- FOR CLEAN UP JOBS * $536.00

-CHARMIN TOILET PAPER- FUN TO CLOG TOILETS AND WIPE WITH * $624.00

-PUFFS KLEENEX- SNOTTY NOSES * $186.00

-DURACELL BATTERIES- NEEDED FOR TOYS, CAMERAS . . .* $325.00

-SWIFTER - FLOOR CLEANER AND DUSTERS- MOPS UP MESSES, ESPECIALLY AFTER EATING AND HELPS CLEAN THE HOUSE! * $270.00 (Hallett's only)

-FEBREEZE- IMAGINE THE SMELLS SOMETIMES! * $96.00

-MR. CLEAN- HOUSEHOLD CLEANER AND DISINFEC-

TANT/MAGIC ERASER *$87.00

-BOUNCE FABRIC SOFTENER- SOFT, CLEAN SMELLING CLOTHES * $102.00

-TIDE LAUNDRY DETERGENT- A LOT OF LAUNDRY * $720.00

-DIAPERS- A LOT OF POOPING * $6,000.00 OUCH!!!!

-CREST TOOTHPASTE- BRUSH TEETH AND PAINT HOUSE WITH * $73.70

-ORAL B- VIBRATING TOOTHBRUSH/ CHILDREN'S TOOTH-PASTE, FLOSSERS AND REPLACEMENT HEADS TO CLEAN TEETH AND HELP WITH SENSORY ISSUES * $200.00

-CLAIROL HAIR COLOR- YOU NEED TO COVER A LOT OF GREY! * $136.00

-SPLASHER'S SWIM DIAPERS- FOR SWIMMING * $360.00

-PAMPERS WIPES –MULTI USES * $160.00

APPROXIMATE GRAND TOTAL NOT INCLUDING TAX, SHIPPING AND HANDLING AND GRATUITIES = $9,872.70

NIKKI: *Three kids in diapers! My family has diapers, Pull-ups, (also know by Sean as "hassles"), all of various colors, shapes and sizes. We have baby wipes, flushable wipes and paper towel by the truckload. Toilet paper must be yummy. Ask my child who likes to eat them. Magic eraser by Mr. Clean Rocks! It helps with all of those scuffmarks and crayon going up the stairs.* **NEED WE SAY MORE . . .?**

17. Carpenter

A worker who builds or repairs wooden structures or their structural parts. (Dictionary Version)

SANDY: My husband is at work a lot so I have learned to become quite the handyman. Of course, that's what I think. Ryan was hanging on the door of the TV armoire and the whole door splintered down the middle. I went out to the garage, got our toolbox and looked for the appropriate tools. I found the drill, unscrewed the hinges, laid the door flat on the floor and got out my carpenters glue. I clamped the wood in place and let it dry for a couple of hours. No big deal right? I then drilled the fixed door back on the hinges. Every time he hangs on that door, I cringe! My other claim to fame would be the back door to our home we replaced. We received a grant to replace our sliding glass door for safety reasons. Ryan had mastered the art of escaping the sliding glass door so we replaced it with French doors. My husband and my nephew Brian replaced the door one Memorial Day weekend. It was done in May and a year and a half later the door still wasn't trimmed out. I couldn't wait any longer for Mike to finish the door. I drove to Lowe's; bought paint; trim, finishing nails, wood putty and a saw. I borrowed my sister- in- law's miter saw. I measured, sawed, hammered, leveled and painted the trim on the back door. It was truly an amazing accomplishment! I am sure a true, red- blooded carpenter would cringe after reading this excerpt but if Martha Stewart can do it, why the heck can't I? Now, no one should call "Better Homes and Garden" magazine. Remember I said I have learned to fix things, I didn't say I was any good at it!! There are many roads to fixing things Nikki and I may not have taken were it not for our kids and our working husband's but I do admit there is such a feeling of pride I receive whenever one of our projects are seen to completion!

NIKKI: *I love Ty Pennington. He's the guy on the show on Sunday nights called Home Makeover. He usually rebuilds a home of people in need. There is usually some tragedy involved like cancer, fire, autism . . . He taught me how to use wood putty and carpenter's glue. I've repaired bookshelves, entertainment doors and hinges. The* *kids love to kick the lower doors on our TV stand. They have cracked the doors, bent the hinges, and knocked the door off. I just put some wood putty in the holes, use some wood glue and clamp the doors back together! I usually use rubber bands, too. Most of the repairs usually last a couple of months. They aren't the prettiest but they work!*

Kiera likes to chew on wooden tables and chairs. It's one of the many types of nourishment she craves. She is the one who bent the hinges on the door, too. We have learned to fix many things over the years. We have repaired wet ceilings from running faucets. We have worked as surveyors for our fence in the back yard. We can also dry wall and spackle walls where things have gone wrong. Even where the computer went in it! You can never have too many home fixing skills when you have children on the autism spectrum.

18. Humanitarian

A person promoting human welfare and social reform.
(Dictionary Version)

SANDY: When I was first referred to Ryan's school, Redwood, there was a waiting list. One of the kids had left for the summer so there was an after school spot for T.C. That way both of my kids could attend the same school. I received a phone call stating a little girl had passed away so now there was a spot for both kids. It was bittersweet. I was happy that my kids would be in their program but so sad for this woman I had never met who lost her precious child. When the kids started at Redwood, Ryan started receiving services through Medicaid. One of the services provided is respite care. The provider comes to your house and watches the child in your home. Usually with respite you have to bring the kids to a particular place. Anyway, one of the first times Ryan had respite I met this amazing woman. She was telling me how she was going to school at the local college. We started talking about Redwood and I asked if she had any children. She said she had a little girl, but she recently had passed away. After talking more, we realized the spot that was given to Ryan was her daughters'. I of course started to cry because I cry at Hallmark commercials, but I was so moved I couldn't believe it. What kind of person can lose a child and then choose to take care of other parents' special needs children. Wow, did she pay it forward! Stories like that always remind me how I was chosen to take this particular path with Ryan.

As a side note, we recently moved to Tiffin Ohio where my son attends a school called the Seneca County Opportunity School. It is the county's MRDD School. Since Ryan first began attending the school, my husband Mike and the player's on the football team at Heidelberg University, attended and played in a fund raising basketball game with local celebrities for the Opportunity school. The football players have also helped to build a playground for the students at the school, too. Whether Heidelberg football has more wins or losses is only one way to measure their success, but helping people with special needs in their community is a much bigger success if you ask me! The cheerleaders at Heidelberg had a fundraiser and made t-shirts that said, Heidelberg loves autism. It was a huge success. Molly, Chris and the others helped raise funds for our local support and education group, S.A.L.S.A. and it helped raise awareness in the community, too.

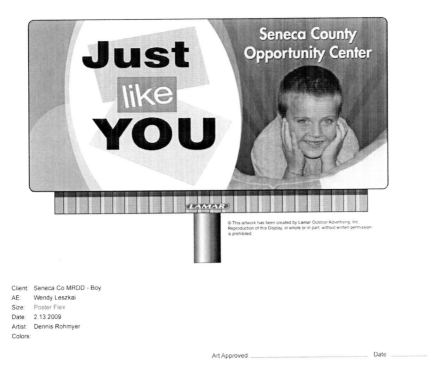

Client: Seneca Co MRDD - Boy
AE: Wendy Leszkai
Size: Poster Flex
Date: 2.13.2009
Artist: Dennis Rohmyer
Colors:

Art Approved _____ Date _____

Seneca County MRDD awareness month billboard on RT. 18 in Tiffin, Ohio

NIKKI: My child has autism, what's your excuse? Order T-shirts on line!
Ok seriously, I cry at everything too. Why do we want to save the world?
My most recent addition to help others was a letter to the local fire department. An EMT had asked for parents with kids with disabilities to e-mail or call him so the dept could help their families better. He has a daughter who is blind so he understands how different special needs are.

> *Dear Steve Jernigan, EMT Hebron, KY Firehouse,*
> *Thank you for your interest and added concern for children with disabilities. Our son is 7 years old and has autism. His safety along with the safety of our other two children is our number one concern in life. We have Occupant with Autism stickers on our cars and house. We did this in case of an emergency and we*

47

were unable to tell rescuers our son has autism. He may appear "normal" because there aren't always outward signs or visible clues of autism. Like most children, they respond differently to each situation. We would expect him to be afraid and panic in an emergency. He may not respond to verbal commands like "Come to me" He may appear as if deaf or that he doesn't speak or understand English. He normally is afraid of new people and in an emergency would be even worse. Try to use short phrases like, "Hold my hand." "Come here", or" I'm here to help you." These phrases may help however not all kids with autism will react the same way. Our son may go with you if you hold his hand. Some children with autism hate to be touched, causing extreme anxiety and may freak out and try to run away flap their arms, scream and cry. Some children with autism do not talk. Some use sign language or pictures to communicate.

Some suggestions for parents of children on the autism spectrum are to watch videos about firefighters. Our favorite is Elmo Visits the Firehouse. It shows what firefighters look like under their protective helmets and Gear so they are not so scary and are only there to help. Another suggestion is to visit local firehouses to see the fire trucks and ambulances. Look at and read books about firefighters, EMTs, and Police officers will familiarize our kids with your appearances. We also can make books called social stories and read them to help our children understand why we need to help firefighters help us. Another idea is to play with firefighter toys, dress up, or have professional firefighters and police officers help our special kids in the event of an emergency not be too afraid. Thank you again for your interest in helping children with disabilities. We are available to answer any further questions you may have. Hope it helped.

Sincerely,
Nikki and Steve Wisor

SANDY AND NIKKI: The Wisor's and the Hallett's have now been initiated in a couple of autism walks. Both families drove to Lexington, Kentucky where the organization "National Autism Association" was hosting a walk. We piled in two cars and drove two hours to pay our homage to autism. Well, it was two hours if we received the correct directions, so actually it took us two and a half hour. We arrived as people were completing the one and a half mile walk at Keenland Horse Park in Lexington, KY. We did end up finishing the walk with Ryan in the stroller, Sean on Steve's back, T.C. and Caley holding hands and Nikki and I took turns with Kiera on our shoulders. All in all it was a rave success. The grand finale was after the walk the kids got to bounce in one of those huge, inflatable bounce houses. Nikki and I were discussing the possibility of a second walk for autism with just the two of us. Our kids had fun but it was a total stress fest. We were all proud to have completed the walk for autism.

The next year was the first annual "Autism Speaks" walk in Cincinnati. It took place at the Cincinnati zoo. Once again the families piled into the car and made the trip to the zoo together. All of the kids participated in spite of the rain. We're hoping to make it an annual tradition for both families to "walk for autism" together.

2007

The NAA National Autism Walk in Lexington, Kentucky
Left to right: Ryan Hallett, T.C. Hallett, Steve Wisor, Nikki and Sean Wisor and in the stroller Caley and Kiera Wisor

T.C and Ryan Hallett at the national "Autism Speaks" walk in Cincinnati

Ryan and T.C. Hallett playing with Caley Wisor and the gorilla statues at the Cincinnati "Autism Speaks" walk

2008

The Wisor family on the merry go-round at the Cincinnati Zoo for the "Autism Speaks" walk in Cincinnati, Ohio Left to Right: Nikki, Kiera, Sean (left top) and Caley.

19. Poet

One who writes poems. (Dictionary Version, Obvious Version)

SANDY: I wrote a poem for my son Ryan:

AWAKENINGS
THE DAY MY SON FIRST LOST HIS SPEECH
I THOUGHT MY HEART WOULD BREAK,
WHEN HE WITHDREW COMPLETELY INTO HIS OWN WORLD,
IT IS THAT I COULD NOT TAKE

I LOOKED INTO THOSE BEAUTIFUL BABY BLUE EYES,
THE ONES' THAT USED TO GLEAM;
IN THEIR PLACE WAS THIS ENDLESS POOL OF EMPTINESS
AND CONFUSION
OR SO IT WOULD SEEM.

AT THE TIME, THERE WAS NO PAIN, OR SORROW OR FEAR
IT WAS AS IF HIS MIND HAD BEEN ERASED,
IT TOOK SOME TIME AND EDUCATION,
BUT FINALLY THESE OBSTACLES WE WOULD FACE.

EVENTUALLY THE LOVE AND PATIENCE OF FAMILY AND
CAREGIVERS
WOULD HELP TO LIFT SOME HAZE;
RYAN NOW LAUGHS, CRIES, SMILES AND POINTS,
FOR THESE THINGS I AM TRULY GRATEFUL AND AMAZED.
WE KNOW NOT WHAT THE FUTURE WILL BRING,
BUT WITH LOVE AND FAITH WE WILL ENDURE,
BECAUSE THE INNOCENCE I SEE WITHIN RYAN
HAS ALWAYS BEEN SO PURE.

WE WILL CONTINUE THIS JOURNEY FOR THE ANSWERS

THAT WE SO DESPARATELY SEEK,
AND PRAY FOR THE DAY TO ARRIVE,
WHEN HE WILL EVENTUALLY SPEAK.

FOR NOW IT'S THE SMALL AWAKENINGS THAT DRIVE US ALL
IN WATCHING MY BABY GROW INTO A LITTLE BOY,
AND WITH EVERY HUG AND KISS I AM CONTINUALLY
GRANTED-
I AM MOTIVATED BY NOTHING SHORT OF PURE JOY.

Ryan Hallett at Aunt Sue's Lake Erie condo in Sandusky, Ohio, 2007

NIKKI: POEM FOR SEAN

A PIECE OF ME DIES
WHEN I HEAR YOUR CRIES;

ARE YOU HURT OR SAD
FRUSTRATED, MAD?

YOU'RE STUCK IN A WORLD
I CAN ONLY GUESS

WHAT IT MUST BE LIKE

Sandy Hallett, Nikki Wisor

TO HAVE ALL OF THOSE THOUGHTS

SWIMMING AROUND JUMBLED
NOT BEING ABLE TO TELL US
WHAT MAKES YOU SO TROUBLED?

WHEN I HEAR YOU LAUGH OR ROAR
IT MAKES MY HEART SOAR!

ALL THE SADNESS AND GRIEF
DISAPPEARS LIKE AN AUTUMN LEAF
YOU WERE HEAVEN SENT
MY BOY
MY ANGEL
MY JOY!

I LOVE YOU MORE THAN THE STARS IN THE SKY
FISH IN THE SEA, SAND ON THE BEACH

TO INFINITY AND BEYOND- THANKS BUZZ

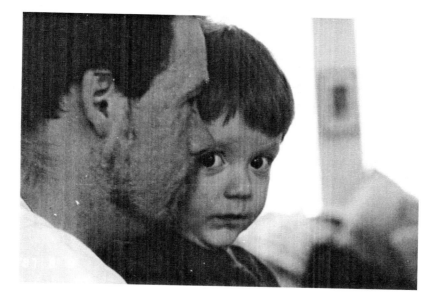

Sean Wisor with his dad, in 2001

20. Insurance Specialist

One who specializes in a particular occupation, practice, or branch of learning of insurance. One who sends out so much paperwork as to confuse the clients? (Dictionary Version and Our Version)

SANDY: Each insurance company has different rules depending on the company, the policy, the state it is in, or if it is a private company. There are so many variables in understanding the laws of insurance. In Kentucky you can be eligible for something called the home-based community waiver through Medicaid. It is based on the child's income, not the parents and it can help a child with autism receive respite care and diapers. There are social security benefits, too, but we were denied for those. Now that we have recently moved to Ohio we had to reapply for Medicaid and there is a waiting list that is decided by each county. We are very fortunate. We must have moved to a county that knows the secret to environmental toxins because in the town of twenty-one thousand residents where I live, I have only heard of approximately six children with autism. I am wondering if I will find the appropriate number of afflicted kids when I go grocery shopping, since the national average is one in one hundred fifty children afflicted with autism.

Since moving to Tiffin and spending some time here the number has now risen to about fifteen kids with autism. Amazing once the word gets out how more people come forward with their child's disability without the negative stigma.

The things that are hardest to know when dealing with individual insurance companies is whether you have to use the in-network doctors for PPO, HMO...IDK (I don't know). I graduated in Art History, not the art of insurance companies. What I can tell you is my son has an eye doctor, a dentist, an Ear, Nose Throat specialist, a family physician (GP), a D.A.N. doctor, a holistic physician, a developmental pediatrician at Children's Hospital, an orthopedist, a physical therapist, occupational therapist, speech therapist, and an MRDD organization called North key and a Medicaid based organization named Caretenders. My son went to a special school called Redwood and Medicaid took care of most of the tuition. Fortunately, Ryan's new school, The School of Opportunity is a county school funded by the state so the tuition is paid for. That is the only thing paid for, though. Our private insurance "specifically excluded" autism services in our policy, until I fought them and won! Sometimes you just have to ask the companies and be persistent for what you need. We now have a specific amount of Ryan's therapies covered.

The first thing is to see if any of those specialists fall under the umbrella of your insurance company. Usually, that would be a negative ghost rider. There are also specific co-pays for each doctor. If you happen to need to go out of town for example to a D.A.N. (defeat autism now) doctor or a holistic doctor all expensed incurred are out of pocket. We had done an allergy test through Great Plains Lab and insurance companies definitely won't foot the bill for those kinds of tests. You have to pick and choose your battles and figure out what will be covered under your plan. If you don't, you can go broke trying. Our B-12 is paid for out of our own pockets, but so are most vitamins.

The best advice I have is never throw any explanation of benefits away! I am still pulling out bills from a year ago and trying to prove expenses to get the insurance company to finally pay! I have very strong legs from my continuous uphill battle!

NIKKI: The state of Kentucky has a law that kids with autism may be eligible for five hundred dollars a month for medical expenses. That depends on WHAT the expenses are and WHO your insurance company is. You have to read every piece of paper from the insurance companies. They will screw you if they can. Can you say- "May I speak to your supervisor?" What you should be saying is "Can you please connect me with your legal department????" Most recently my doctor wrote a letter telling my insurance company that the ADOS (autism diagnostic observation scale) test for my daughter was medically necessary to diagnose her autism and that for them not to pay it would be medically negligent. You see the test was billed as speech therapy and our company doesn't pay for speech therapy unless you get an injury that causes you to loose speech. Make sense? Of course not!!!! That's why the insurance companies are rich and we are getting second mortgages and our credit cards are at their maximum limits. I have personally de-forested the rain forests with the mountains of paperwork we have from insurance companies.

21. Painter

One who applies paint especially as an occupation.
(Dictionary Version)

SANDY: My son doesn't have a lot of hobbies at this time. He also doesn't really like to pretend play, which is typical for kids with Autism. One of his favorite pastimes is to watch movies. He does connect with Walt Disney's Pixar characters' Buzz Lightyear and Woody. In the movie Toy Story there is a favorite part where Buzz Lightyear flies off the stair railing, flies down the stairs and lands on the bottom with a broken arm. Ryan loves to take his Buzz Lightyear toy and fling him down the stairs to the bottom. There are plenty of other toys that have followed, too. The floor and walls are destroyed on our stairs, because of the nicks in the paint. I guess you could call that pretend play?

Our living room has a hammock swing in it. When Ryan becomes over stimulated he goes over to the swing and he swings in it. For example, if he is visually over stimulated by Toy Story he may seek out his swing. It is fantastic that he knows how to self modulate. The only down side is he loves to bang into the wall and the back door REALLY hard. We have had to fix the dents in the wall and repaint the wall and door. We are actually in need of another coat. We paint nicks a lot. Always keep a lot of back up of your original paint colors. Ryan also leans back on kitchen chairs, which in turn scrape off paint. About a month ago, he was playing in the den and he tore the curtain rod out of the wall, anchor and all. Mike and I finally got around to fixing the hole and painting the patch of wall. We choose very earthy, neutral colors. One day, my friend Pam, and her daughter Mariah were visiting. Mariah came in and asked if it was OK that Ryan was eating peanut butter. I didn't think anything of it at the time, but when we finally looked into the kitchen it looked like the apocalypse. I had left a jar of peanut butter on the kitchen counter and he had opened it and decided to paint the kitchen walls, the table and his body with the whole jar of Jiffy. Needless to say, we painted our living room and Den the colors of a neutral brown. The color appears to be a mix of colors between peanut butter and poop. We figured camouflaging the wall couldn't be necessarily a bad thing!!

Ryan painting peanut butter on the table and walls in our kitchen, 2006

NIKKI: My husband has to do a bit more traveling than we'd like, however, when he's away I try to do something to surprise him when he gets back. I'm constantly using Mr. Cleans magic eraser on the walls and up and down the stairs. I finally got sick of cleaning and decided to paint the walls to hide all of the marks. I was trying to hide the pencil marks, crayons, fingerprints, markers and chalk. I also have to paint for sanity reasons. I'm an artist at heart. It brings me peace. I painted the kids upstairs bathroom like it was an underwater world. It has a matching shower curtain and there are fishes hanging from the ceiling. I also painted a chair rail going up the stairs to hide all of the fingerprints and hide all of my "little Van Gogh masterpieces."

22. Sleep Depreivation Specialist

One who specializes in a particular occupation, practice, or branch of learning associated with sleep studies. One who learns to live on a few hours of sleep a night. (Dictionary Version and Our Version)

SANDY: When you have a child the first thing you give up, as a parent, is sleep. Remember back in the day, sleeping until noon the day after a late night out with your friends? Oh the good ole days! The difference between the before kids era and now is your typical newborn's sleep pattern eventually works out their day and night schedule so you sneak in those extra couple of naps you were missing previously. When you have a child with autism your sleep, or lack of sleep I should say, is a definite issue. It continues well into adolescence. Most of these kids lack the melatonin (the hormone that brain manufactures to produce sleep) used to help them sleep. We spend a lot of time outside getting as much fresh air as possible. We limit naps at school because otherwise Ryan won't sleep through the night. At age six our biggest problem is when Ryan wakes up at three a.m or four a.m and we don't hear him when he goes in the family room, turns on all of the TV's and lights and tries to make himself a juice cocktail with whatever he can reach in the refrigerator. Two hours later you wake up, go downstairs and realize your refrigerator light has gone off because it has been open for hours. From outside our home it looks like there is a constant party going on! Our neighbors must think we are crazy! Different solutions have been advised from our physician. There are some sleep aid alternatives such as clonidine. We are just sticking to the melatonin for now. There is only one problem. Ryan won't chew up pills so sometimes we have to put them in his sippy cup. He will fall asleep relatively easily but that doesn't necessarily mean he stays asleep. Our newest problem is, if the cup stays near him while he is sleeping and we don't dump it, he sometimes drinks from the same cup the next day without us realizing it. He may fall asleep at school if he drinks it in the morning or after school if we don't find it. For now, we just live with our six or seven hours of sleep at night or less and learn to live with it. I do feel bad for Ryan at times when he can't sleep. I know he is frustrated and wants to sleep at times, he just can't.

NIKKI: Please don't say to someone "How do you do it?" when they tell you they've had only two hours of sleep the night before. Chances are they are a pro at functioning on little to NO sleep at all. In ye olden days, before we knew about melatonin, it would take about two hours to get Sean to go to sleep. I would bribe Sean with a whole bag of popcorn and a movie to get him to lie in bed in hopes he would finally fall asleep.

When Caley came along I had to do the same thing with her. She had thirteen ear infections and no sleep either. She would wake up crying every hour.

Sometimes I can be so tired I forget how to sleep! Once asleep, who knows how long it will last? I usually have to lay with them to get them asleep. It is not abnormal, though, for my children to wake up at three o'clock a.m. to go downstairs and watch TV or play on the computer. That's why we all sleep in the same room. Our hope is we will hear someone wake up and this way we can get them to go back to bed. Kiera is a little better when it comes to sleeping but not by much. I'll catch up on my sleep later in life.

23. Fashion Designer

One that creates and manufactures a new product style or design. A person who "garanimalizes" their children in soft, tag less apparel that is not made of sensory defensive materials. (Dictionary Version and Our Version)

SANDY: A long time ago I was one of those parents that were so picky when dressing my kids. The styles and brands had to be cute and have name brands. Well, that changed rather quickly. The amount of clothes we go through in a day is a world record in itself. Having a "husky" kid limits you to styles of clothes. We wear a lot of t-shirts and sweatpants. The pants are usually too long to match his waist size. Do you remember "Welcome Back Kotter" for all of you forty something's? Well my kid is a sweat hog. He sweats sleeping, walking, jumping. That also limits his wardrobe. Ryan has something called Sensory Integration Dysfunction. The sensory issues are very common for kids with autism. He is very sensitive to tight or itchy clothes. If you put him in a turtleneck you may as well put a noose around his neck because he acts like he is suffocating. Shirts with tags that itch, forget about it! Sweatshirts on a cold day may work, but if it is a "hoody," (a sweatshirt with a hood) the neck hole is generally too small so he appears to be very uncomfortable. Talk about torture; try getting that thing back off of him! His cranium is rather large! If you put long sleeve t-shirts on him he usually chews on the cuffs or the neckbands. When I pick him up for school there are usually small holes accompanied by huge puddles of saliva on his clothes. (It's an oral thing!) Last summer we outgrew swim diapers. Anytime you have a larger child, that is most likely going to happen, but the potty training thing is usually an issue, too. You can't go swimming without a swim diaper for safety and hygiene purposes. I researched swim diapers like I was getting my PHD and swim diapers were my thesis. First of all, the cute baby suits with the diaper built in are for kids weighing about twenty pounds. My kid already came out at ten pounds four ounces so I already had a head start. The diaper I found I like the most is the KIEFER swim diaper. It is white and for kids and small adults to wear it under a normal, everyday bathing suit.

That takes away his fashion stigma at the pool for having special needs, but they can wear a sporty swimsuit on top of the diaper.

NIKKI: *Sweat pants that are one hundred percent cotton is what Sean likes to wear. If it's not one hundred percent cotton he will break out in a rash and overheat. It's like his skin can't breathe. It's weird but it's true. Temple Grandin, for those unfamiliar with her, is a brilliant PHD who invented the hug/squeeze machine. (It is a machine that controls pressure around the body that decreased the anxiety in animals and people.) She has autism and has written many books on the subject. She once wrote, "what her mother made her wear was painful." She was referring to certain fabrics that were scratchy or stiff. Funny the things you remember? Besides all clothes that are made from one hundred percent cotton, we used to dress Sean in overalls to keep his hands out of his pants or his goodnight "hassle". Tag less shirts. AMEN!!! God Bless the person who created the tag less. It must have been a MOM!! As I mentioned before Kiera's fashion sense is quite absurd looking but I need to keep her out of her diaper. I put her "onesie" outside on top of her pants so she cannot get in her diaper. Caley had the same issue at two years old but thankfully grew out of it! Her problem now is she too wears sweats or leggings because jeans are not designed for five year olds wearing pull-ups. Then there's the whole problem of buttons or snaps that they can't work.*

Anytime we leave the house and go to the playground, I always had Sean wear red, bright green, orange or yellow shirts so I could spot him quickly. Just in case he decided to bolt. You'd think the beautiful auburn hair would be enough, but I guess not. Now that we have three kids, I at least try to keep all three in the same color shirts. For example at "Chuckie Cheese," this summer, they all had matching green shirts. Caley had on a hibiscus headband from a luau this summer, hot pink lei, rainbow tights with hearts, and a primary colored floral dress. Hard to miss, don't you think? She dressed herself. Kiera had the same colored shirt with a gingham overall short's outfit and a balloon tied to her back. That was also easy to spot. Sean also wore the same colored green T-shirt so I could keep track of him, too. Some friends and family have mentioned ironing their kid's shirt or pants for school. I am mildly amused knowing my kids are always dressed comfortably either in sweatpants or shorts and almost always t-shirts. They deserve some comfort right? This is at least something I can control and provide comfort.

24. Bus Driver

The operator of a motor vehicle used for transporting children to or from school or on activities connected with school. (Dictionary Version)

SANDY: The key to driving your kids to and from school is to keep them amused. Whether you are taking just your kids to school or chaperoning other kids to a school function, you need to play a lot of music or games that they like! Some young children like CD's like Kids Bop, Disney or specific songs playing on the radio. You just need to find something they enjoy. I find the drive is always less stressful if I play their music compared to mine. Every day on the way to school the kids and I listen to the radio instead of music. When we lived in Kentucky we would listen to a local radio show in Cincinnati. It's on the radio station Q-102. The morning personalities are Jeff and Jenn. Jenn Jordon's son Jakob has autism. Jenn is a huge advocate in the Cincinnati area. She even has a play date set up the second Saturday of every month so other kids on the spectrum and their parents have somewhere to meet. It's very cool. T.C. also thinks it's interesting anytime he hears someone on the TV or radio has autism. He says, "They have autism like Ryan."

Besides the variety of music and radio shows you need a car, van or sports utility vehicle big enough to accommodate a zillion car seats, booster seats and gear. The laws keep changing in regards to car seats, but last I heard the child had to be forty-eight inches tall and eighty pounds? Can't that be a little skinny seventh grade girl? My mother only weighs approximately ninety pounds. Also, I'm not one of those parents that don't let their kids eat in their car. I tried that once. The first day I brought home my new VW Passat, it had just been coated with something so it wouldn't stain. "No eating in my car!" Those were my famous last words. It looks like I was eating my words and they were eating in my car! My kids always seem to be hungry, and if we snack in the car it makes the trip seem shorter. I find they get grumpy if they don't eat after a certain amount of time. If it will make the drive easier I'm all for it. What did we do before snack packs; juice boxes and fast food were invented? Starve in a really clean car I'm guessing.

Ryan getting off the bus from the Opportunity School in Tiffin, 2008

NIKKI: I have to drive the kids in the minivan to many different appointments a day. We have occupational therapy for both Sean and Caley. We also have speech therapy for both, too. Sean has physical therapy he attends privately; on Saturdays Sean has play therapy. Most recently Kiera has been getting therapy and that has been added to my bus-driving itinerary for the week. After all things are said and done we spend all five days of the week after school attending over fourteen therapies for three children. With all of this driving of all the kids to their specific therapies we also have swim lessons at the YMCA or parenting classes. You get the picture how I may feel like a bus driver. By the way, I don't stop at railroad tracks, open the door and listen for oncoming trains.

25. Dishwasher

One who cleans dishes, kitchen, food preparation equipment, or utensils. (Dictionary Version)

SANDY: We not only go through a lot of laundry, we go through a lot of dishes too. Thank God there is the invention called the dishwasher. Ours is so overused it doesn't drain correctly anymore. Most of it drains and then I take the turkey baster to get the rest of the remaining water out. Classy. Besides the appliance we also have human dishwashers. Not a sweatshop worker but very hungry kids that want to be a part of the clean plate club. For example, when T.C. is eating chocolate cake and ice cream, he will physically lift up the plate and lick it clean. He also does that with the other food group, ketchup. Not to mention he spilled so much milk after eating cereal I started buying those bowls with the straw attached. Ryan doesn't usually leave many morsels behind, either. His way of cleaning his plate is to turn the plate upside down and dump the crumbs on the floor. He does that or runs his finger in the bowl. I guess you would call that-finger licking' good. Either way it gets the job done. We always use those divided cafeteria plates for dinner, but I think I am going to start buying the divided paper plates and paper bowls. This constant loading and unloading of the dishwasher is starting to annoy me. Do you ever feel like a hamster on a wheel? First you make breakfast and dinner, load the dirty dishes in the dishwasher, run the dishwasher, and then empty the dishwasher. You see where I am going with this- a hamster on a wheel, constantly running!

NIKKI: All three of my kids love to play in the dishwasher. I suggested that we call Fischer Price and have them design a kid's size model for kids to play with. There is nothing more fun to my kids than opening and closing the door especially if the bottom rack is out. CRASH!! There go all of the dishes!

Sean recently has started turning the dials and imagining that it's the control panel from Mission to Mars from the cartoon shows "The Backyardigans". If I were smart, I would remember to turn the switch off at the wall under the cupboards. That would be too easy. There are too many other important things to do.

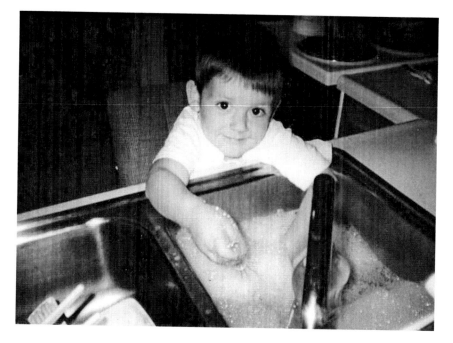

Sean Wisor washing dishes, 2000

26. Fireman

A person who tends to fires and fire safety. (Dictionary Version)

SANDY: One thing that I find difficult is trying to emphasize the dangers of fire and fire safety to Ryan. How do you tell a child with autism not to touch the hot stove so he understands? We leave the light on in the oven so he can watch the food cook; otherwise he is constantly opening up the hot oven. I have an anxiety attack every time I am boiling water on the outside burner. When we first moved to Tiffin a blister showed up on Ryan's chin after dinner one night. We figured out he had opened the stove and set his chin on the hot door. He has such a tolerance of pain that he didn't even cry. How scary is that? We have many smoke alarms in the house but if I burn food and it goes off, it only annoys Ryan. He may stand in the middle of the room and plug his ears, but it does not really scare him. We make sure to put the alarms and special locks with chimes on doors and windows, too. So far, he does not seem concerned about the windows. He doesn't really show fear in a lot of situations. He is a climber, a jumper and he has an oral fixation and chews on many things. He mostly fixates on chewing on electrical wires. I guess it has the perfect texture he likes. They tend to be the perfect texture like a "chewy tube". He has chewed through our computer mouse, video games, DVD chords. . . It's a lot cheaper and safer for us just to keep a lifetime supply of aquarium tubing around the house! I hope that some day we can get across the urgency of danger to Ryan. It is just a little scary to know he is not afraid of anything, except for the dragon on the movie Shrek.

Since moving to Tiffin, we did a fundraiser for autism: "Give autism the boot". The money raised helped people in our community and northwest Ohio. The firefighters helped us by parking their fire truck and using their boots to collect money in. They were so helpful. Is it a coincidence that most firemen are hot?

NIKKI: *I never thought I could come up with a story for this occupation. I was going to use the horrible story my Mom would tell us on everyone's birthday. Don't get your hair too close to the candles on the cake. It might catch on fire, like my cousin's did when I was a kid. Her face melted. Nice image, huh? However, I found myself saying the exact same story this year when Caley leaned into her birthday cake! Sean did singe his hair one year, though. So I continue preaching on the etiquette of candle blowing for the birthday cake. Hair net possibly?*

The other day, Kiera decided a box of matches looked yummy to her. I caught her chewing on the end of the box of wooden matches. They were hidden but somehow she found them. The fun just never ends around our house. This Christmas she also tried eating the Christmas lights off of the Christmas tree. All I could picture was the poor cat that fried in National Lampoon's "Christmas Vacation" with Chevy Chase. He plugged in the Christmas tree lights and cremated the cat that was chewing on the electrical chord. Jeez, no wonder my doctor and therapist think I need to be on medication! I'm just warped!

27. Pest Control

One who exercises restraining or directing influence over pests. (Dictionary Version)

SANDY: We live in a neighborhood that used to be farmland. Needless to say we get some critters around our house. Because of the eating habits of Ryan I am very obsessed with trying to avoid bugs in my house. That and I am not a huge fan of bugs anyway. I think I would flip out if I got ants or roaches. They would have to commit me! They could easily eat off of the crumbs on our kitchen floor or living room cushions for a year. Of course I am anal retentive and try to clean the crumbs as often as possible but you know how supply and demand works!!! We don't see too many bugs but we have a pet chipmunk that likes to live in our garage sometimes. I also believe we have moles in our yard. That can't be good. The two things I can't stand most are crickets and spiders. Flies are nasty, too, but the crickets and spiders infest our basement in the spring and fall. I'm one of those people that can't stop obsessing about the loud cricket in the basement until I kill the darn thing. Now the other issue is the spiders. I can deal with Daddy long legs; it's those huge- hairy wolf spiders we get. Yikes! I spray in the basement and around the perimeter of the house but I worry about the chemicals hurting the kids so I use an organic bug spray. When our nephew, Adam, came to visit one time, we saw a humungous spider in the front of our house and freaked. I was looking for a rope so I could lasso it with when we told Adam to kill it! He ran over to it cautiously and stepped on it. He squished the spider but about one hundred baby spiders seeped out and scattered in every different direction. It was DISCUSTING! He went running for the hills!

NIKKI: In the Cincinnati area you get an invasion of cicadas every seventeen years. It may be one of the most disgusting things ever witnessed. The local news channels covered the infestation a couple of years ago when it happened. It was on every channel and you would have thought it was the locusts from Armageddon. We were preparing for the swarming locusts. We were battening down the hatches and clos-

ing our windows, too. We were terrified for Sean because he hates loud noises! Sean doesn't like a lot of bugs either. He's afraid of houseflies, too. These cicadas were big, loud and would fly in swarm when they were buried in the earth to wake up every seventeen years. Other parts of the states get little doses of the nasty cicada every summer so you don't get that horror film scenario. When the Cicadas finally did come, Sean wasn't as effected as we would have thought. Not that we were playing outside during the infestations. He never did touch one of the cicadas but Caley did. **She even tasted it!!!** *The swarm was revolting but not as bad as the millions of dead carcasses stuck to trees and lying in everyone's lawn. Some businesses in Cincinnati were even dipping them in chocolate as a delicacy. I should have brought some home for the kids to try for dessert!*

28. Midnight Grocery Shopper

One who buys groceries when the other parent is home and kids are asleep to avoid public meltdowns. (Our Version)

SANDY: After the many grocery-shopping escapades with Ryan's meltdowns, I try to avoid grocery shopping with kids like the plague. Of course my husband is one of those people that work about eighty hours during the football season. You have to find one of those grocery stores that are open twenty four hours and have everything you need in one stop shopping. One of the last time's I went grocery shopping with the kids it was a nightmare. You see, Ryan weighs about seventy-five pounds. I used to pick him up and put him in that front compartment of the cart. You know that part where they sit with their little skinning legs hanging down? Ryan is too tall or heavy for me to lift him in and out of the cart. Instead, I choose to put him in the basket. You can see how this may impede how many groceries I can fit in the basket. The other thing is, every time I put something in the basket Ryan would try and open it up and eat it. When I would say no he would scream and throw a tantrum the likes I had never heard before. You would have thought I was sawing his arm off. Of course there were plenty of people staring at me because I couldn't control my child. That was the icing on the cake. They didn't know the half of it. It can be difficult at time because our children appear "typical". They may come off disobedient or sometimes aloof, because they don't like to look you in the eye. I have had people in the check out line ask him his name. When he ignores them I feel the need to explain he is non-verbal, not rude. You would be shocked at the amount of people that comment to him how lucky he is to just sit and enjoy the ride. "Why don't you get out of the cart and help your Mommy" different people have said. Then of course my inside head voice would say, *"why don't you mind your own business?"* That comment was to me, I hope. I can't always shut that mechanism off.

NIKKI: Midnight shopper? Maybe on E-Bay, that is. I've never been awake enough to leave the house at midnight. I usually fall asleep around 8:00 PM when the kids go to sleep. I also get a good amount of catalog shopping in the bathroom, too. Our grocery shopping routine is generally a Saturday morning thing. Steve is home from work and the one-person shops for the food for the week while the other one watches the kids. Sometimes one child will go but to take all three kids is a nightmare. It's just too difficult when they're all together. How many carts would that take- six?

SANDY AND NIKKI: Someone was ingenious and printed a card to hand to nosy people in stores. You can buy them online and a website called buttons and more. It reads: "My child has autism. He / she are not being naughty and we are not being bad parents for not reprimanding them. Children with autism can often behave in an unpredictable manner, because they find it hard to cope with many everyday situations. They are quite simply doing their best. Please be patient. For more information about autism please visit www.autism-society.org. What a spectacular idea! It can be very frustrating while you and your children are in public and your child has a complete meltdown. It took some parent out there that had to tell one too many people their life story to get them to leave them alone. Hats off the mother of all inventions! Amen to "necessity is the mother of all inventions!"

29. Bathroom Attendant

One who attends a service in the bathroom. One who watches over to make sure the water is turned off, the sink is not flooding and the water bill doesn't exceed the national debt. (Dictionary Version and Our Version)

SANDY: To be a bathroom attendant you would think that means to be the attendant in the bathroom, wouldn't you? I know you imagine me standing by the door, towel draped over my arm and a tray of cologne for Ryan and T.C. to choose from. No really, we're just kidding. The problem with Ryan is he spends most of his time going to the bathroom- outside of the bathroom. If his pull-up is too wet, he takes off his clothes wherever he is. If he has a "code brown" he usually goes in the corner for privacy. (With his pants up, thank God) We have had some very bad bathroom days. Some days have begun with the night *overflow* in the "goodnights pull-up." After that, you have to change all of the sheets on the beds he wet. Ryan has been known to be a sleepwalking nomad so that would include a minimum of three beds. There are never just one set of sheets to change in the morning. This morning, when he pooped, his first version was to wipe it on the carpeting. As my husband changed him I spot cleaned the carpeting. Later in the day, he wiped his poop on his shirt. Fortunately that is a little easier to clean up. I know what you're thinking. Why aren't you watching him closer? It's because he is sneaky. He will only poop and wipe if he's by himself for a couple of minutes. We go through more pull-ups in a day. It's because he holds the world record for number of daily bowel movements. Don't get me wrong; he eats a good amount of food in a day, but not enough to justify the amount of crap he excretes. OK, you're not going to believe it. He did it again!!! There goes another diaper! I caught him this time before the famous wipe though!

I know I may joke a lot about feces, but how else should I handle it? There is nothing more embarrassing than finding your child playing in his excrement when you have company over in your home. How do you explain poop smearing to family and friends if not through laughter, than through tears? I will opt for the latter.

NIKKI: Our powder room has a lava lamp, puzzle, a game boy, a potty training Elmo that drinks, talks, and sits on the potty, potty books and of course Clorox wipes! We have posters with the whole 12-step program for the bathroom:

1. *OPEN DOOR*

2. *TURN ON LIGHT*

3   *PULL DOWN PANTS AND UNDERWEAR*

4. *SIT TO POOP AND STAND TO PEE*

5. *WHEN FINISHED, CALL MOM (IF #2, WIPE, NOT SHAKE)*

6. *PULL-UP UNDERWEAR AND PANTS*

7. *TURN ON WATER*

8. *WASH HANDS WITH SOAP*

9. *DRY HANDS*

10. *TURN OFF WATER*

11. *TURN OFF LIGHT*

12. *CLOSE DOOR*

SIDEBAR: We are not picky about the whole toilet seat or lid issue and there are corresponding illustrations for all twelve steps.

Our bathroom is not the typical bathroom in everyone's house. Ours have potty books, DVD's, cars, a TV tray, cars, and music. We're very supportive of Sean going potty. We prepared for "Potty Fest 2005". We had heard of a weekend potty training for kids who have difficulties learning how to use the potty. After finding out it was three hundred to four hundred dollars a weekend, we decided to do it ourselves. We used naked pictures of what to do, step-by-step instructions on the wall so Sean knows how to go on the potty. We are still potty training at age nine! We just hope when people come to visit they don't think the pictures on the wall are child pornography. A lot of kids with autism need visual cues when helping them learn a new task. The most helpful thing we did was put him on Paxil. His obsessive-compulsive disorder and anxiety were preventing him from using the bathroom.

The famous flooded bathroom in the Wisor household!

30. Physician

A person skilled in the art of healing and medicine.
(Dictionary Version)

SANDY: OK, not to be a buzz wrecker but some of this book needs to be informative, too. I am not a doctor and I don't claim to play one on TV. Ryan was born in 2001. He is now eight years old. When he had so many illnesses as a child, I requested a copy of his medical chart. It appeared to me it was the size of the novel War and Peace. Yikes! I wanted to see his vaccination schedule and see if there were any environmental clues as to why our son was diagnosed with autism. I know I have learned more about antibiotics, vaccines and other medicinal subjects than I care too. My son was born two weeks early, C-section, healthy apgar score and a head with a circumference of 14.49." (Ouch!) In the first two years of Ryan's life he had twelve ear infections, pneumonia and chronic bronchitis. The ear, nose and throat doctor finally opted for tubes in his ears. He was on a cycle of various antibiotics: "Omnicef, Biaxin, Floxin Otic, Augmentin, Amoxicillan, Cipro and Phenergan." He was also vaccinated with all of the appropriate vaccines: DPT, Polio, Measles/ Mumps/ Rubella, HIB, Hepatitis B, and Varicella vaccine for Chicken Pox. This totals approximately fifteen shots in less than seventeen months. By the time all was said and done, he was two and showing signs of autism. His chart stated we were beginning to discuss behavioral issues right before his birthday. At two, his head circumference was 20.08 ". *What did that kid on the movie Jerry McGuire say? The human head weighs eight pounds? No way, that can't be every human head!!!*

Being a Catholic I tease and say that's why I have the guilt. (See # 72) It is true. If I had to do it all over again after reading the previous paragraph it seems obvious to me what happened, but 20/20 hindsight is a luxury I am not entitled to. I believe genetics plays a part in autism, but that does not rule out environmental factors or a strong catalyst when your immune system is compromised.

After being diagnosed, we stopped Ryan from drinking cow's milk, started giving him supplements and were put into a program in Kentucky called

"First Steps". The state diagnoses the child and helps with therapy and services until they are three years old. One of the hardest memories I have is watching videotapes and remembering how Ryan used to look at us and speak with simple words. Then one day he regressed into this little boy who would stare at fans and lights and not say a word. He felt no pain and he had no range of emotions. They say it is like their souls were stolen when they became autistic. Whoever says that- knows. It is the total truth. Today, Ryan is rarely sick and will look at you smile, laugh, cry, hug and kiss us. He is still non-verbal and doesn't speak but he makes some great sounds and does some sign language. He also gestures and uses a communication device. He is a loving, happy child who reacts more appropriately to pain and emotions. We are truly grateful for the small things.

After Ryan's diagnosis I read a lot. One of the things I never knew was autism can be a symptom of something much different physiologically. We had Ryan tested for a chromosomal analysis for Fragile X. It came up negative. We did many other tests like an EEG for seizure activity. Ryan was born with a white spot on his abdomen that never tans. We just figured it was a birthmark like any other. Our physician Dr. Mark Deis (who we adore) told us it could be a sign for something called tuberous sclerosis. It turned out it was not that. Other tests performed were about four hearing tests, a vision test, blood work, and urine and stool samples. Parents tend to do a lot of this testing to get answers. Obviously, part of the reason I did this is because I was not ready to fully admit that my son had autism and maybe, just maybe, if it were some other explainable, physiological disorder it would be easier to cope with. Fortunately, I got off the denial bus and jumped in headfirst once I admitted my son had autism.

Today we were initiated into the family of the emergency room takers. Yes it is hard to believe that in Ryan's six years of life, today was the first day we had to take him to the hospital. What a nightmare! Ryan was jumping on his therapy ball and he came up hard and hit his head on the corner of the dresser while watching TV. It was a head injury so you can only imagine the amount of blood! My whole family took him to the emergency room. We explained how he has autism, he has a high tolerance of pain and he is non-verbal. What I guess that means at our hospital is wait right here and we'll be back in two hours so try to occupy your time constructively. To all of you parents out there you understand waiting in the emergency room. You watch the clock as it ticks by in dog years. We were finally helped, but we were told the gash in Ryan's scull would need to be stapled or stitched. We opted for the choice not given, glue. Can you imagine the obsessing with loose strings or metal parts on the skull of an autistic child? After another hour and a half we took Ryan home.

Ryan, 1 and T.C., 2 (notice the head size), 2001

NIKKI: Why else do they call it "medical practice"? When dealing with the illnesses of children with autism it takes a lot of trial and error and guesswork. Our little angels can't say, "My ear hurts". So you learn to diagnose the illness by the symptoms. For Sean, if his ears look dirty, it must be an ear infection. If they feel like they're on fire, it must be a fever. Obviously some symptoms are a lot easier to figure out then others. If the child is lethargic or vomiting, call the doctor. If they have a fever over one hundred two degrees; you can probably use the Tylenol suppositories. If there's also diarrhea it could be a little more difficult to figure out. Most children with autism have intestinal issues and don't necessarily have regular bowel movements like typical kids. It might be something they ate or it could just be a bug they picked up. Literally. I won't even get into the midnight nail cutting and splinter removal part of being a doctor.

31. Social Director or
Socially Unacceptable Director

A coordinator of events either acceptable or unacceptable in nature. (Dictionary Version and Our Version)

SANDY: It's very important for children with autism to be introduced to social settings. Autism is a social disorder. Kids may parallel play but they generally prefer to play on their own. Sometimes I think Ryan pushes his boundaries at school so he can be placed in time out. That's what his teacher tells me anyhow. I think she may be right. Speaking of social, it's difficult for children with autism to understand boundaries or socially unacceptable behavior. In one of Ryan's phases he would take off his pants and diddle himself. He would do this at school, home; in the car . . . you name it. I mean, I am a woman, so I don't get the whole infatuation but he sure loves that thing. He'll walk around with his hands permanently down his pants. You tell him no, but it goes right back in. He tends to hug you real hard on your leg for deep pressure, if you know what I'm saying, like Rover. There were actually times I would pick Ryan up from school and there would be packing tape around his waist because he wouldn't leave his sweatpants on! Fortunately that habit has gone to the wayside. Eating boogers, now there is another hobby. I think he prefers to have a congested nose because of the salty treats. I don't know how to break him of these habits. I know all kids have their issues; it's just they usually stop when you tell them to. I think my favorite is when he has gas. Wow can that kid fart! I'm sure that ties in with his gastrointestinal problems, but he doesn't understand in public not to let them out so loud and stinky. That can be embarrassing. Oh well, as the French say, such is life or C'est la Vie. I have learned to have a very thick skin if people want to judge kids for being kids. Not just special needs children but all kids.

NIKKI: *At the YMCA it is socially unacceptable to be naked in the pool. That of course doesn't stop Sean. We are not supposed to bite into Hershey bars in the check* *out lane at the supermarket. That would include the wrapper and all-of course, but that doesn't stop us either. We don't believe in screaming in church, so we just stopped going. We don't put our hands down our pants in public. Well, at least we aren't' supposed to.*

Sean once walked up to a man at McDonalds and took a French fry off of his tray. Thankfully the guy was friendly and said to Sean," I hate waiting for my food too". Another fun time was when Sean was with my Dad and me at the store. There was a long line and patience isn't one of Sean's virtues. I asked my dad to take Sean to the car so he didn't have to wait for the line to go down. My Dad tried to get Sean into the car, but he started screaming uncontrollably! We were getting looks galore! I hope no one thought he was being kidnapped!

Grocery shopping can always be an adventure. Caley had a meltdown at the store one time and screamed for over an hour at the grocery store, Bigg's. (For those of you not familiar with Bigg's it's a hypermarket with fifty or so aisles) We try not to shop with the kids very often. Countless people came up to us and asked what was wrong with her. I ended up just taking her and Kiera to the car while Steve finished shopping with Sean, who, for a change, was behaving very well.

32. Shoe Salesman

One who is employed to sell shoes in a store. (Dictionary Version)

SANDY: We all have certain outlets to help us cope with our problems. One of mine is buying shoes. I admit it! I have a slight fetish. I like to shop for shoes like it's my job! I inherited that trait from my mom. My dad calls her Imelda Marcos. I love my shoes. The only problem with this habit is I have a size ten shoe and toes like Fred Flintstone. I inherited those from dear old dad. Thanks dad. My husband Mike, and our neighbor, Jamie, likes to call me "Yabba Dabba Doo" when I'm outside in sandals. They say it in the same tone as the "robot" (from the Fred Flintstone cartoon episode when Fred is cloned by a robot.) Aren't they hilarious! Well, needless to say, my son Ryan not only inherited my physically unique toes but his feet are fat on top, too. This makes it virtually impossible to find shoes for him. Add in the sensory integration dysfunction issues, and my son will not leave his shoes on no matter what the weather. It has just been brought to my attention that my neighbor is buying me shoes for my birthday since I'm barefoot a majority of the time- like my son. That is in spite of my vast shoe collection. He also says I am giving people in Kentucky a bad name by never wearing my shoes! Maybe that's where Ryan gets it! Isn't it ironic? I like to go barefoot but in my closet I counted sixty-five pairs of shoes. Ouch, my slight fetish has turned into a full blown "issue". Oh well, the shoes help me as a coping mechanism. When it comes to Ryan, I have spent countless hours and many dollars trying to find shoes not only to fit Ryan, but also to get him to keep them on. We have tried leather shoes, tennis shoes or sandals; ones with Velcro, ties, zippers, and bungee stretch bands, slip-ons or canvas high tops. We just can't find that miracle shoe my son will leave on. Maybe that should be our next project!!! Never guess what I did this weekend? Yep, I bought a pair of leather high top basketball shoes for Ryan. (They were on sale so I could justify it!) Ryan got to school and his teachers got a good laugh out of it. They have seen more shoes on Ryan. He came in, sat down and his teacher Tiana asked Harriet to time how long it takes Ryan to take off his new shoes.

Less than two minutes. I understand why he needs to take off his shoes in the home and the car, but school? Oh well, there has to be that perfect pair of shoes out there for Ryan to keep on his feet and for me to help fulfill my fetish. Until I find them, I will continue to shop! It's my duty after all. If the choice is comfort food or shoes- I choose shoes!

*NIKKI: I love my babies' feet! For some reason when Sean was a baby, I remembered reading somewhere that it was harmful to children's feet to wear shoes before they were one year old. At that time Sean's shoe size was **XXX Wide**. He had the cutest, chubbiest, fattest feet! Sean didn't get his first pair of shoes until well after he was 1 year old. His feet were so chubby (how chubby were they?) They were so chubby that they just didn't fit into any shoes. He was one and a half when he actually started wearing shoes. It was wintertime and I bought him a pair of sandals from Gymboree. They were of course out of season and on the clearance rack. They were the only things I could fit around his plump feet. The next year we actually found him some weather appropriate shoes; some snow boots. Shoes are still a problem today for my kids. They would prefer to be barefoot most of the time. It doesn't matter if it's hot and sunny out or if there snow is on the ground.*

Caley went through a unique shoe obsession/phase that she only wanted to wear the same pair of Elmo and Zoe sneakers. She would cry and throw a fit if she couldn't wear those shoes. It didn't matter that they had holes in them, or were filthy, or were too small, or even wet. Transitions are very hard (quite an understatement) for our kids, trying new things, especially shoes, and is next to impossible. I have to guess their shoes sizes. I have to imagine what designs they will like. Sean is a creature of habit. He would still be wearing the same pair of Gerber baby shoes if they made it in his size. I can't tell you how many shoes I have purchased and had to return because he flat out refused to wear them. He doesn't/ can't do laces, so I have to find Velcro or elastic sneakers for him. As he grows this is becoming more and more challenging to locate. Thankfully, his feet are freakishly small compared to his size. His friends T.C. and River wear sizes three and four in boys. Sean is just getting to size two. He has a few inches on T.C. and close to a foot taller than River. He is at least twenty-five to thirty pounds heavier than both boys. Kiera had the most adorable pair of boots ever. They were pink suede with pink fur lining. I picked out a pair similar to my Ughs (knock-off Uggs from Australia) for her. She wore them ALL the time and was quite styling in them. She cried when she pulled them out of the box and they didn't fit her feet anymore.

I am the opposite of Sandy and hate buying shoes for myself. I was at a sporting goods store trying to buy sneakers and no one was helping me. I was having an anxiety attack because I couldn't find my size, price range, or style. Sandy had to talk me through it.

33. Biochemist

A person who deals with chemistry and chemical compounds and processes occurring in organisms. (Dictionary Version)

SANDY: It is amazing the things you read and learn about when your child is diagnosed with autism. There is the D.A.N. protocol, chelating, supplements . . .I could have never predicted that I would be scraping poop from a child's diaper and shipping it to a lab for heavy metal and toxin analysis. Who knew? One of the theories for autism causation is the thimerosol in vaccines. Thimerosol is a mercury based compound used as a binding agent for various vaccines. One example is the measles, mumps and rubella shot. I believe this could be one of the many pieces of that large unsolved puzzle they call autism. In my opinion some of it has to be environmental. We sent Ryan's blood and urine away for various tests. A year after my son had his vaccines he needed another series of them. I was definitely not having any part of that. I am not opposed to vaccines in a healthy, non-predisposed child. How could I justify a child dying of polio when they have a vaccine to cure it? I haven't received proof autism is caused by vaccines but I definitely haven't received proof to the contrary.

Besides blood tests we also had urine analysis, hair analysis and stool samples. That was a lot of fun. We tested for urinary peptides, food allergies and bacteria abnormalities and heavy metals. He tested positive for lead, cadmium, arsenic, aluminum, and mercury. These tests were both interesting and informative. We were trying to figure out why my son never had a solid bowel movement and why certain things were happening to him- was it because of what he ate, drank or touched. Scientists say second hand smoke contains arsenic and cadmium and the metal aluminum can be from food in cans. We also found out he has a sensitivity to casein and milk based foods. We were on the Gluten/ Casein diet for over a year to see if made a difference. It was subtle so we now modify his diet somewhat, but he is still the champ of diarrhea!

NIKKI: Children with autism usually have a hard time taking medicine so you have to get creative. We used to pulverize the medicine in a coffee bean grinder. The bottom of pint glasses work really well for smashing pills, too. We've also tried rolling pins. Any of the above will work.

Figuring out how to break down a pill is only one problem. Once it's crushed, what food shall we hide it in? You had to keep changing the choices of foods because Sean would catch on pretty quick. Sometimes we would hide the medicine in his applesauce or chocolate pudding. Now our favorite is in his breakfast granola bar. I guess the chocolate chips mask the medicine flavor. Deciding how to break the pill was one problem. Deciding which food to camouflage the medicine in was another problem. The biggest dilemma was which food do you choose to put the medicine in because the texture of food chosen to hide the medicine had to be just right or Sean would vomit. Obviously, if there were vomiting involved, you lose all of the medicine too. Now what do we do? Give it to him again or call it a night? Fortunately more companies are making better-compounded medicines that taste better. There are chewable pills, and shots are quick and easy as a last resort.

34. Actor

One who represents a character in a dramatic production.
(Dictionary Version)

SANDY: What's that saying, "never let them see you sweat?" Well obviously you never carried an eighty-five pound kid on your back, up a hill. (In the snow, barefoot, both ways . . .) Talk about sweating!! One of the difficult things about kids is how darn smart they are. Kids with autism are very perceptive children, even though they may not always show it outwardly. Ryan is very smart. If I am having a crabby day he seems to sense it. Those are the days I try to mask my crabbiness under my veil of acting. It doesn't always work. I try to be cheerful and fun most of the time. Now you know I am an actress! Ryan may not understand acting or appropriate play, but my son; T.C. has one of the most vivid imaginations of all time. He does skits with his friends and plays with his action figures with full sound effects. That is another skill he learned from his proud mother! Hopefully some of that imagination will rub off on Ryan, too. Ryan is not a huge fan of acting or pretend play. That is pretty typical for people with autism. For Halloween we dress him up, and take him out. He never would have gone if candy weren't involved. He has been a Disney character for Halloween almost every year- it seems to be what he recognizes the most. I have him pick out his costume by seeing how enthused he becomes at the store when walking down the costume isle. Year to date he has been Tigger the Tiger, Winnie the Pooh, Buzz Lightyear and Woody from Pixar's Toy Story, Mike Wazowski from Monsters, Inc. and this past year he was Mr. Incredible. (I second that!) We have picked most of his costumes because of his recognition and because they are loose fitting. He won't wear a mask or a costume made out of itchy material. He definitely won't wear a hat or a hood. We tried that with Buzz Lightyear one year. It was a complete debacle. His sensory issues made it a "not so enjoyable" evening of trick or treating so we took the hood off. He does like it when we take him in the wagon while he sits back and eats candy. I mean, come on, who wouldn't enjoy that! He used sign language for the first time this year. I couldn't have been prouder.

Ryan as "Buzzlightyear" and T.C. as the "Incredible Hulk", Halloween, 2002

NIKKI: It's always "Showtime" with my kids. You never want to let them see you sweat! Smile, Smile, Smile. My son Sean is quite the little actor. He directs us in his own productions and tells us what to say. "Mommy says". . ."Daddy say". . . "Caley say'. . . "Kiera say". . .

On Presidents Day last year Sean had to stand up in front of the whole school wearing a paper beard and sing songs with the whole class. I never would have thought he would have done that in a million years. One teacher stood in front of the kids prompting them with the words while Sean's teacher stood behind him bribing him with m&m's. T.C. stood next to Sean to help. He did a great job until it just became too overwhelming and then he plugged his ears and came down from the bleachers to get a little alone time.

35. Confidant

A Person in who one confides information to. (Dictionary Version)

SANDY: When dealing with problems I vote for A.) Therapy; B.) Antidepressants; C.) Alcohol or D.) Talking things through (or E. all of the above). I find talking things through helps me to process the issues I am dealing with. It's great, as your kids get older, you can sometimes become friends with your kids' friend's parents (say that ten times fast). Two of my closest friends are the mothers of two boys, River and Sean (Mom is co-author). These are strong, energetic women that communicate the same way I do. That would be fast, discombobulated and a definite SEGUEY FREE ZONE. We joke about this because when people witness our conversations it is hard for the layman to follow a path of logical conversation. The three of us speak almost daily. Between the three of us we have regular play dates at our houses. There is a two year old, a three year old, two four year olds, two seven year olds and an eight year old. All of them have varying degrees of personality traits, of course. We have a blast! One year I had a birthday party for T.C.'s friends, their siblings and the Moms' only. Yes, cocktails were involved. That is the only way to throw a birthday party. Let the kids trash your house; feed them more sugar and self medicate the Moms' with some wine. Good idea indeed! I am a talker and so are they! I enjoy the sisterhood of talking with other women that have similarities and histories with myself. My sister in law Jo is my "rock". I also have my family, my high school friends, my kid's friends and my life long friends. You all know who you are. They are how I cope with the everyday surprises my kids have for me, and they help me find the humor in life. I have a bad habit of always trying to cover my pain and guilt with sarcasm and humor but my friends, through years of translation, have learned to read between the lines and see I actually wear my heart on my sleeve.

NIKKI: *The only autistic person I had ever heard of was "Rain man". The proverbial nail in the coffin (My therapist is cringing right now!); Nancy was my best* *friend since childhood. She had researched autism after many play dates and discussions about our kids. Her son Connor is two months older than Sean and she knew despite Connor's milk and peanut allergies, he was developing typically and Sean was not. Nancy is like family, and it must have been so difficult for he to bring up the subject of autism, but she did. I don't remember the exact words but coming from her I knew there must be something wrong. Have I ever thanked her? I can't imagine what she went through before I got there. We had set up play dates. We ended up moving to Kentucky when Sean was eighteen months old, and I ended up seeing her more then. Before Sean was born I had already picked out the best day care for him. The daycare we went to, which was the most expensive and the closest to my work. We set up schedules with Bud's work and my work. What is that they say about the best-laid plans? I worked up until my due date and past it. After the kid's were born I have stayed at home to raise them. I'm lucky to have a handful of really good friends, especially my husband Steve. When he goes out of town on business my brain is not functioning at it one hundred percent capacity.*

36. Dancer

A person who moves or seems to move up and down or about in a quick or lively manner. (Dictionary Version)

SANDY: When Ryan was young I used to hold him up and spin him around like we were dancing like Fred Astaire and Ginger Rogers doing the waltz. Ryan loves music and appears to have good rhythm. When we play music he sways back and forth and sideways to the music. I don't sway; I tend to nod my head to the music. You may call me a typical "head banger" dancer! We call Ryan's swaying "The Frankenstein". His Grandma, Marly, does a similar shimmy. Mike is the good dancer of the family. Unfortunately, T.C. takes after me, the poor child. Do you remember the show Seinfeld? Well, T.C. dances a little like Elaine Bennis. We tend to sing to Ryan to calm him down. He likes to take our hand and do hand over hand arm movements as he sways to the song. When we do the ABC's we have an extended dance version. We make up special moves and jive the song up some. We have always made up funny dance moves for him so hopefully his dance moves will continue to get better with time. Maybe some day I can take a lesson from him!

NIKKI: We limbo, mamba, salsa, anything to make the kids laugh. With the song "Twist and Shout" Kiera does the best. "HMMMMMM, I know, jump front, jump back, clap, clap, clap, march-march-march, slide to one side, slide to other YEAH! It was from Mickey Mouse clubhouse. Daisy's Dance- (Donald Ducks wife) it's too cute! Sean was watching the movie "Hitch" with us when Kevin James did the dance for Will Smith "start the fire, make the pizza, arms are always moving, Q-tip Q-tip, throw it away. It was hilarious! We never saw the end of the movie because we kept on dancing with him and laughing. In the summer we worry maybe the neighbors will think that we opened a nightclub or karaoke club. We sing at the top of our lungs. God Bless TIVO.

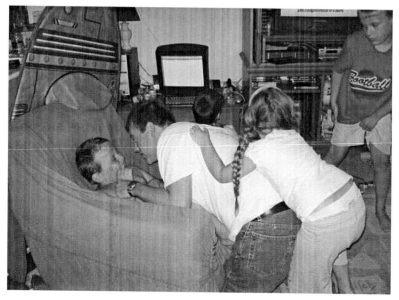

Steve and Caley Wisor dancing and singing with Ryan and T.C. Hallett, 2007

37. Pharmacist

A person who compounds or dispenses medicines.
(Dictionary Version)

SANDY: My son was put on a lot of vitamins and supplements from his D.A.N. doctor, the nutritionist and his holistic doctor. He was told to take taurine for antioxidant function and melatonin for aid in sleeping. He used enzymes to help with digestion, cod liver oil, and omega three and omega six compounds for essential fatty acids for brain food. The list goes on. Endura Guard, a peptizyde, which helps to break down specific proteins such as gluten and casein which he, has sensitivity to. Vitamin C, IgG 2000, calcium, magnesium and B6 have been proven to help some kids with autism. Probiotics were given for the good flora in his gut and so were many other vitamins like A, B, and C. (Maybe that's where that song came from. NOT!) I got a lot of his supplements from a place called Kirkman Laboratories. They are online and make a good product, mostly gluten and casein free, if needed for the diet. They have something called Super Nu-thera. It is a multi-vitamin in powder, liquid or caplet. We tried the liquid ourselves and it was vile. There was no fooling Ryan either for he was utterly disgusted. The powder was OK, but I would suggest the caplet if you have strong enough flavors to cover the taste. The smell was bad enough. He was a good boy for drinking some of the nasty concoctions I made for him! Ryan gets some minerals and vitamins but in simpler forms. For a fruit and vegetable supplement we now use a vitamin gummy used from whole foods. It has a few servings of each and since it is in a gummy form he will tolerate those. We can't get him to eat hardly any whole fruit or vegetables, with the exception of a few baked potatos and occasionally a few baked beans. (With brown sugar and bacon, of course!)

When Ryan was first diagnosed we went to a specialist and had all of the above vitamins and minerals prescribed for us. You tend to reach for any answers when your child is diagnosed with autism and you don't know which way the treatment will lead you. We still use vitamins and some supplements but we have weaned him off most of the other things. He is a happy and healthy boy for the most part and we keep introducing him to the vegetable and fruit food group but to no avail. We spent a lot of money trying new things and some of them worked and some of them didn't. The best advice I have is to find other parents with children with special needs and ask them what works best for them. Don't' forget some children with autism have similar eating habits but no two kids are exactly the same.

NIKKI: When I was young and I was sick, my parents would take me to the doctor and I would get medication. I was a very "sickly" child. I had to take a lot of medication. My husband Steve, on the other hand, grew up in a household that believed medication was secondary to letting the immune system handle itself. His family rarely needed to go to the doctor.

When I started having children I stocked up the medicine cabinet with fever reducers, pain relievers, allergy medicine, band-aids, syringes, nose swabs . . . I had everything for any unknown illness. When the time came and my children needed medication, Steve and my different opinions regarding pharmaceuticals became an issue. Making the decisions to medicate our children wasn't an easy one. Both Dr. Manning and Dr. Deis felt it was necessary to prescribe an anti-anxiety medication to ease Sean's stress for potty training. I believe it took us months to actually fill the prescription. When we finally did we gave him the lowest dose possible.

38. Computer IT Specialist

Someone who repairs and fixes computer network problems and trouble shoots computer issues. (Dictionary Version)

SANDY: Hard Drive? What's that? I'm just kidding. I'm computer illiterate, well almost. In college, we just started using computers. We still used electric typewriters to type our papers. Man, did I just age myself? Using a computer begins in preschool now. Ryan and T.C. began in the same preschool class three years ago and they had a computer they both used. Ryan is not as efficient as T.C., but he can manipulate a mouse and a touch screen. Of course, when I say manipulation he can also throw the keyboard on the floor, continually turn off the computer so we have to re-boot it and unplug wires I would have no clue what to plug it into. Our computer is in our den. We keep our collection of CD -ROMs Ryan likes to take out of the drawer and scatter around the floor like flower petals. It's funny how he loves chaos and disorder, but after he gets a snack out of the cupboard, or a toy from a drawer, he always has to shut the door or drawer, because it will drive him crazy. One day, when I came to pick Ryan up from school, his teacher Tiana asked me to sit down and watch Ryan on the computer. She turned it off, then on again and we watched as it was rebooted. When the icons came up he chose one from the fifteen options and touched it on the touch screen. He then cancelled and picked certain programs to get to the one he wanted. He led us through approximately six screens to find the one he wanted to play with. It was one of the most amazing things I've ever seen. I knew my son was in there, but he was REALLY in there! I had never seen him solve the puzzle of navigating computer programs before. I now watch him, Sean, and T.C. on the computers and I am utterly amazed every time!

You should have seen the computers Nikki and I used for this book. Talk about archaic! It would have probably been faster to write this book on the old electric typewriters we had! We couldn't even e-mail it to each other because the book was too big. I tried to e-mail it from Heidelberg University and we crashed their computer network. Needless to say, they were not very happy.

NIKKI: I am a computer idiot. If it was not for my husband, I couldn't even check my e-mail. Steve is probably regretting now that I found E-Bay. (Just kidding Steve.) When Sean was one, he started using the computer. When he was three, Sean had locked us out of our computer and changed file names and moved them. It was amazing! He also logged into his preschool teachers e-mail at school. It's fun to watch Sean on the computer, especially when we are visiting family and using their computers. Caley will still sit and watch him play on the computer, and now Kiera will, too.

Do you know hard it is to explain to your grandfather how e-mail works? My Dad still doesn't understand the concept of cyberspace. When he sends me e-mail and I'm not on on-line to receive it, he wonders how will I get it? I might as well be explaining the Hynsburg's Uncertainty Principle to him. I could explain it to him one thousand one times and he is not going to get it.

The Wisor living room where you can watch a movie, play Playstation, play on the Wii, work on the computer and Tivo the show you're missing! 2008

39. Interior Designer

One who practices the art of planning and supervising the design and execution of architectural interiors and their furnishings. (Dictionary Version)

SANDY: How to balance a sense of style in a house of chaos. That is the question. I spent my first two years of college studying interior design. I like to think I have some sort of style, but it is hard to maintain when you have children. In our old home we had a "therapy" swing in the living room. It is one of the biggest conversation pieces when people come to visit. We have a new sensory gym in the basement I just completed. It is similar to the one we had in Kentucky. It has a mini trampoline, a sit-and-spin and other apparatus on a foam floor. The foam flooring is blue, green, red and yellow in a bright pattern. We still need to hang Ryan's two swings in our basement.

The Sensory Gym in Ryan's basement, Tiffin, Ohio 2008

I like my kids to enjoy their toys but I don't want to see them everywhere. They have their own "spaces" in their rooms for toys. I also built those pre-fabricated bookcases and drawers in the den to hide a lot of the toys. I use it for the toys and for my glass collection. Yes, you heard me- I collect glass. My minor in college was glass blowing and Grandma Marly still blows glass. I have them all set out on shelves around the house. I know what you're thinking. It is the perfect collection for the kids! Amazingly enough, Ryan generally leaves the glass on the shelves alone. I also have the many photographs my father has taken. My parents are world travelers and they share their eye for composition and the love for exotic places with us. Those are on the wall to add to the design of the house. I wanted to have a home that was comfortable for people to visit, artsy enough for my style, and colorfully fun.

NIKKI: What color of paint will hide the poop stains on the walls? What other colors will hide the fingerprints, chalk, marker, pens and pencils. If you are reading this book chances are you either know someone who has a child with autism or you have a child with autism. If they are coming over to visit for any length of time . . . GET HARDWOOD FLOORS! Either that or invest in a really good carpet steam cleaner.

I'm a big fan of slipcovers. We have slipcovers on almost all of our furniture. We have a lot of hand me down furniture that we just put slipcovers on and we put blankets or comforters under the slipcovers to make them more comfortable! We also have slipcovers on our kitchen chairs. Imagine the amount of food that spills on those chairs. They're easy to wash and dry the same day and put them back on. I picked the cotton twill kind because some of the kitchen chairs are a damask material and they don't wash up very well. The basic purpose of my interior designing is to camouflage the stains or rips in the furniture or décor. Another favorite of mine are area rugs. It's an inexpensive fix to cover worn or stained carpeting.

40. Acceptance Speech Writer

The people surrounding our families- and ourselves-supporting us physically, emotionally, mentally and sometimes financially. (Our Version)

SANDY: Thank you for accepting the personal shout outs- specifically people that have helped us in our support network. From the time the kid's were young, I was blessed with a helpful family and giving friends. As the years go by, and the challenges become greater, it is more difficult to find the time to take a break for yourself. I want to thank all of the people that have helped our family, especially the people who hosted overnight excursions, because it is not always easy. The first time I left Ryan for weekend was a trip to Chicago with Jo, Bruce, Sue, Mike and I. My parents and my sister, Sue, watched my children for me. There was also the time when my dear mother-in-law died a few years a go, not only did my parents and my sister, Sue, watch the kids but also held a special "balloon" funeral to honor grandma and help them understand she was in heaven.

I flew to Chicago with T.C. for Tiffany and Marc's wedding. Our friend's Lenny and Holly took fabulous care of Ryan! At my twentieth year reunion, one of my dearest friends, Jill, had her husband Kevin watch the boy's overnight. He was terrified but he did me proud. They had the time of their lives!

It is difficult to entrust people with our children. Not because they are not trustworthy but maybe a little because of my "martyrdom". It makes it difficult for me to ask people for help. I can count on two hands how many times I've left my children overnight. Thank you Amy for watching Ryan over the summer and Molly for being part of my family in Tiffin- I can't thank you enough. Thank you Jenny for my much needed weekend away in Florida. Thank you to all the caregivers, babysitters, family members, doctors, teachers, therapists and friends who have loved and taken care of my children as their own and to help give me a greatly needed break.

Thank you, most of all, to my husband Mike, for being the best dad to our children, for being the best husband and for being my best friend.

Barbara Streisand, "People, People who need people-are the luck- iest people in the world."

NIKKI: I had respite service (someone to watch our children while we weren't there) for two years before I used it. It required sixty hours every six months to use, but we had a minimum requirement we needed to meet. I never used it because it was hard for me to trust people with my children.

The idea of respite is to leave the house to take a break. When respite would show up I would go upstairs to do laundry and clean, but never leave the house. My friend Sheri had the same respite services and she recommended a woman she truly "trusted" with her child. Her name was Kathy. I called Kathy and arranged for her to come watch my children. I have never felt so comfortable with anyone in my life. (Besides Sandy, of course!) Until that point Steve and I had never left the children alone with anyone since we moved to Kentucky. It wasn't until we actually left the house that we felt secure enough to relax with someone else watching our children. Kathy was not only someone to be trusted; she was a "godsend". She is like a surro- gate grandmother. My kids and I adore her!

I wanted to thank the academy, but I don't mean the pediatric academy . . . just kidding, I wanted to start by thanking Kathy and her daughter Cassie for the amaz- ing care and commitment they have made to my family. Thank you to my sister Grace, her husband Scott and Josh and Nick for their patience and hospitality every time we visit- they welcome us into their home as if it is our own. Thanks Uncle Dave for letting us put you out a couple of times a year at Christmas time. Thank you for going the extra mile to make sure Sean has all of the comforts of home. Thank you Kathleen, Kyle and Allison for allowing Sean to hog the video games. Grandmother Jean, even know you haven't been able to lift Sean since he was one and Grandfather for allowing the kid's for playing the saxophone, naked!

To Aunt Anna for giving us the most memorable beach vacation at her home in Cape May; for being Sean's godmother, and never expecting any less from him, in spite of his condition. Of course, the rest of our family and friends for going out of you're way to make our visits comfortable and enjoyable.

I want to thank my parents who gave me a safe, loving and stable family. We traveled all over the world; they exposed me to fine arts, fine foods and fine people. They helped me become who I am today. I only hope I can do the same for my children.

My mom left the earth in 1991, (no she wasn't abducted.) She's never met my beautiful children, although I know she watches them from heaven. She instilled in me my beliefs, that I can do anything. My mother's strength is one quality I strive towards, especially since my house will never be as immaculate as hers. My children will always be confident if I have anything to do with it.

My husband Bud, I love, adore and admire you. You are my rock that keeps me grounded. I could never have done this book or anything without your love, support and silliness. You remind me daily why I fell in love with you and wanted to start a family with you. At times you drive me crazy, but I also know the feeling is mutual. Your strength pushes me through the tough times and you bring levity to the most uncomfortable situations.

41. Psychologist

*A person who studies the mind and behavior in relation to
a particular field of knowledge or activity.* (Dictionary
Version)

SANDY: A lot of kids with autism have behavioral issues. Some like to be left
alone, some hurt themselves and some can be violent to others. Some are all
three. There are great programs for children with autism. There are programs in Kentucky for the Mentally Disabled and Developmentally Delayed.
Places like Holly Hill, North Key of Northern Kentucky, and Redwood
Rehabilitation. Places in Tiffin like the Opportunity School and Sentinel
"help me grow programs. Many states have different programs. There is also
ABA therapists, or behavioral therapists that can help with behavior. My son
is a pincher. Sometimes it's because he is aggressive. Fortunately you know
when its aggression because it's written all over his face. This would be a
good time to avoid him. Other times he is pinching because he is trying to
be funny or tickle you. Obviously we try to look at his body language and his
cues. He doesn't have very good fine motor skills and he has trouble holding
a pencil or food utensils but when he grips your skin he can instantaneously
bruise you. It feels like he is ripping the flesh off of your arms. I did try to
get some program through a state agency called "Impact Plus" but it never
really happened. The psychologist asked me to sign a paper that stated she
thought my son was moderately mentally retarded. Not mild or severe but
moderate. One thing I can tell you is just because my son is non-verbal; it
doesn't mean his mental facilities are moderately retarded. I would not sign
the papers because I did not agree. These psychologists test children on a
case-by-case basis and I did not agree with her findings. That's all right; nei-
ther did his doctors or therapists for that matter. Needless to say, I am still
waiting to hear from this agency.
  One day I met a woman who was on the panel of therapists and psychologists where my son was diagnosed with autism. It was over three years
ago when he was diagnosed. This woman asked my son's name. She recognized it and asked if my husband was a college football coach. I asked her

how she remembered our case specifically? She smiled and said, in a politically correct way, that my husband has never been forgotten because of his "passionate" response to the panel that diagnosed Ryan with autism. She remembered *where* Mike told them all to go and *where* they could put their diagnosis. She was not rude in any way when explaining this to me. Because of Mike's reaction, the panel learned not only of Mike's unconditional love for his son and his passion for fatherhood, but that day they learned more about sympathy and empathy. I remember that day like it was yesterday. We were both very upset to say the least. I was crying and Mike was angry. He can be a little intimidating at times if he is upset. His physical stature is six feet, five inches tall and he has more expression on his face and body language than most people do. They not only told us that Ryan had autism, but they put it in writing which makes their decision so final. It was one of the hardest days of our family's life.

NIKKI: It can be very frustrating when your children don't speak or can't tell you what is wrong. They can't articulate their feelings and you have to get into their brains and try to figure out what is wrong with them. Is she hungry? Maybe that is why she is irritable. Is he tired? Is that why he is so crabby? Maybe they're not feeling well and they don't know how to communicate that. Are the noises too loud? Is that why he is yelling and plugging his ears or is it because he is frustrated? Are the fluorescent lights bothering their eyes? (Fluorescent lights appear differently to children with autism and it irritates their eyes). Some verbal people with autism have said the lights are constantly blinking and strobing. How horrific does that sound?

Sean for the first time last month told me he needed to go to the doctor. I asked him why and he says, "your ear hurts." That was huge for him to be able to tell me where it hurt. I take care of everything for them. The laundry detergent to the cups they like to their favorite spoons, shirts, and the way to cut their sandwiches. I also need to know the difference between their hurt cry, mad cry, frustrated cry and of course their fake cry.

When we asked professionals for quotes on our book, my "life coach," Allyson Blythe said: "Nikki's humor and energy keep me on the edge of my seat. We can all learn a lesson or two from the loyalty and devotion she has for her children."

42. Recreational Therapist

A person trained in methods of treatment and rehabilitation in the recreation field. (Dictionary Version)

SANDY: I like to take the kid's to the park near our house. The park has typical things for my kids to play on, swings, a balance beam, slides and many other things to climb. We also go to the park when we visit my family. We have to make sure Ryan climbs up the ladders and rock walls for a while and he gets plenty of slide time when we're at the park. On this one weekend my family and I took the boys to the park. We went with Aunt Sue and Grandma and Grandpa. We had Ryan climbing up many different ladders to get to the slide. My problem is I can be one of Ryan's biggest limitations. I see an obstacle, sometimes when I get scared for him. My Mom suggested Ryan should try a variety of ladders at the park and guess what? He did a phenomenal job! I sometimes forget his limitations and I may add more. Don't forget to keep encouraging those kids, unless of course they do the "Superman" impersonation. Then you should probably limit them. If my Mom had not suggested Ryan to try different things on the playground I would never have known his progress- thanks Mom.

One of the most inspirational situations experienced was something my sisters did. My older sisters, Kathy and Sue, got together and wrote a grant for a special needs playground in Columbus, Ohio. Kathy is a landscape architect in Columbus, and works for the parks programs and Sue is an occupational therapist. The two had an idea to build a playground, and they did! To quote my sisters' paper:

Playgrounds are more than just a park with climbing apparatus that provides sensory stimulation for children. A playground can be a refuge for the whole family. We want to share the following vignette that comes from the experience of the first author to illustrate the meaning of playground play for one family.

As an occupational therapist, I have always understood conceptually the therapeutic value of playgrounds. Playgrounds offer a place to play and the sensory stimulation necessary for children whose central nervous systems are developing. As an aunt, I have watched my sister take my nephew to the playground everyday and I see that the playground provides much more than sensory stimulation. At the playground, my nephew, aged 4, who is diagnosed with autism, can participate in the meaningful occupation of play regardless of his limitations. My nephew doesn't care that the playground provides him with needed sensory stimulation. He likes to go to the playground because it is fun. He likes to go because he can swing, run, and slide with his brother. From the moment that he enters the playground until the time that he leaves, both he and his brother are smiling from ear to ear. They both love the playground. They both get upset when it is time to leave. While for my sister, the playground provides a refuge - even if it is for a short time. It provides a place where she can go and just have fun with her two boys. She can forget about all those issues that are associated with having a son who is "challenged." The playground is one of the few places where she can look into her son's eyes and he looks back laughing and smiling. She can understand what he is feeling and why. It is one of the few places where her two sons can play together as if nothing is wrong. They can play and interact just as she had always dreamed that her sons would. And, for just a moment, her grief, guilt, anger and frustrations melt away. So much is communicated on the playground, but not a word is spoken. For that brief time, nothing else matters but the joy of watching her two sons playing together - in the formal language of OT, they are participating together in a meaningful occupation.

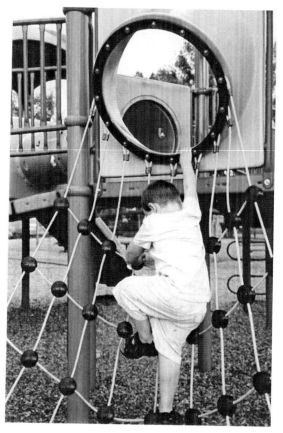

Ryan climbing a rope ladder at Woodland Park in Perrysburg, Ohio 2006. "Yes they did build it and they did come!"

NIKKI: It is fun to have fun with your children but you have to know how to have fun with them! Thanks "Cat in the Hat" by Dr. Seuss. We make play therapy trips to the YMCA. We like to go swimming as a family. We also get on the trampoline and jump a lot. It is one of those fifteen feet trampolines with an enclosure. We have the trampoline and the swing set in the back yard we all like to play on. We also have a couple of different swings hanging in our basement. We have a sock swing and a regular swing. We also have a couple of beanbag chairs and beach balls they play with. We encourage the kids to play with cars and trucks down there. It is not unusual for them to ride their bikes and scooters down there, too. The basement is unfinished so there is a lot of room for the kids to play with their toys. The cement walls are like an empty canvas for their masterpiece-they take chalk and draw beautiful pictures or games on the walls.

43. Book Restoration Specialist

One who specializes in a particular occupation, practice, or branch of learning in fixing books. (Dictionary Version)

SANDY: Some kids have different compulsions. With autism, they are just amplified slightly in some kids. My son Ryan has a disposable book collection. This in turn means my whole family has a disposable book collection. I think he is weeding out the tastiest of the books. Ryan likes to chew on books, eat the book covers, tear out the pages and sometimes ingest the paper. I think he likes the texture of chewy paper in his mouth.

We use a lot of "Kentucky silver" in our house. To the layman, that would be duct tape. If duct tape doesn't work- Elmer's glue, super glue, packing tape . . . any old tape will do. You can imagine what some of the bindings of our book collections look like. It's hard to read them in a bookshelf with no name on the binding and it looks pretty tacky, too. If the book is too badly torn we just pitch it in the garbage. T.C. has his favorite Dr. Seuss book collection he has had since he was a baby. They have taken a real beating. Ryan was relentless with those books. Some of the books are missing covers and some pages are gone. It makes it rather difficult to read a book when there is no ending to read!

The moral of this story is don't start to read a novel and leave it on a table for Ryan to ingest. If you can't finish it in a couple of days, you probably shouldn't start it in the first place. The up side to that is my speed-reader skill have become much faster over the years.

NIKKI: God bless packing tape! When it comes to book restoration there is an art to packing tape. I use it on EVERYTHING! That is unless Kiera decides she wants to eat it. Then I opt to fix the books at a later time or date. We have a huge inventory of books at our house. The kids love to read and look at the picture books. I have repaired hundreds of the kid's books, their puzzles, toys, boxes, dollhouses and game boards with packing tape. There is one note of caution I must share with you, though. If there are pages in a book that get wet or worn the kids may decide to tear out the damaged pages of the book. People with autism and Obsessive- Compulsive- Disorder don't generally like the look or feel of the damaged pages. Because of the disorder they may also have a problem leaving wallpaper or wallpaper border alone once the adhesive wears off. They will pick at the paper until the surface is smooth. They can be pretty relentless.

Just recently, our family was at my sister, Grace's house. Sean was in the bathroom for an unusual amount of time. When we found him he had peeled over three-quarters of the chair-rail border off before we caught him. I was mortified! My sister handled it very well. She thought it was time to redecorate anyway.

44. Photographer

One who practices the art or process of producing images by the action of radiant energy and especially light on a sensitive surface. (Dictionary Version)

SANDY: Most of my family has great photographers in it. They use high tech cameras, point and shoot cameras, digital cameras and/or a movie camera. They take a lot of pictures at family events. I rely on them for our printed memories since school pictures and studio pictures are not the best option. Most children with autism won't look at a camera. Ryan didn't used to, but he will now smile for a camera, occasionally. Our first and only public photography experience was at a JCPenney department store a couple of Christmas' ago. It is difficult to get all kids to sit still long enough to get their picture taken. Imagine taking a child with autism for the first time to a studio for a whole session of holiday pictures. To quote my husband, "it will be a cold day in Hell before we ever do this again." I believe he said graduation pictures would be the next time. We got to JC Penney's and of course they were backed up. It was hot in the studio and we had to amuse the kids for an extra forty-five minutes. You can imagine how easy that was! The JC Penney catalog really isn't that interesting to keep children occupied for an hour. Thank God for the back of the catalog showing the toys. We almost had enough time to write out Santa's list! We finally got inside the studio, sat the kids on this box with the sheet behind them and proceeded with our appointment. When T.C. would smile, Ryan would fidget. When Ryan would smile T.C. would look away. One would move out of the picture while the other would start moving their mouth. The woman photographer thought it was a great idea to get them to laugh so she was making really loud noises and cackling. This didn't make Ryan laugh it just annoyed him. He was plugging his ears and looking very agitated. Mike had to hold them both in the picture so they would cooperate. We did finally get one print out of thirty pictures. You can still see Mike's hand on their backs holding them up. I guess that's what makes the picture so great. Considering he never used to look into a camera and now does, it made for an ever-present moment. It was a great example of "a picture's worth a thousand words."

NIKKI: *There's something about taking a picture that brings me such joy. I guess it may be proof that we are happy, and it reinforces that despite our challenges. We are just like any other family. I have THOUSANDS of pictures all over every surface of our home. We have pictures on our refrigerator, our front door, walls, disks and checkbook cover. They are everywhere! I also have a ton of scrapbooks and albums, too. PECS is the Picture Exchange Communication System- we use a lot of these for Sean's communication. It is a system where a person will exchange a picture for something they want, a place or an action in substitution for their words. We use them in something called a picture schedules. This is where you plan out your child's day in sequence by pictures. We also do social stories, so we have always taken tons of pictures of Sean. Pictures are snap-shorts of happy moments. We treasure them just like any typical family.*

The Wisor Family at Christmas in Burlington, Kentucky, 2008

45. Teacher

One whose occupation is to instruct. (Dictionary Version)

SANDY: I commend anyone that can teach. I adore my kid's teachers. I have been very fortunate in that regard. The important thing I've learned is whatever the kids learn at school needs to carry over to home. It is especially important with autism because of a child's routine. When the occupational or speech therapists give me homework I try to incorporate it at home. Repetition and reinforcements are very important. When they were working on computers at school we got a touch screen for home and that helped. When Ryan works on puzzles or line drawings at therapy we would do them on the weekends, too. At times it can be difficult to gauge age milestones when you are working with a delay of any kind so you try to be on the same page as all of the other educators in the kid's lives. One of the greatest stories I heard was from Ryan's teacher Tiana. When I would pick up Ryan at school, I would give him a piggyback ride. He would open the door by using the handicap button and we would leave together. As Ryan and I were leaving, I commented on how we would all have to be careful with the entrance since Ryan knows how to get out. She told me when Mike drops Ryan off in the morning, Tiana comes out and gets him and Ryan punches in her 4 number security code to get in the building. I was amazed! Not only did she teach him to open the door with the code, but she never had any doubt he couldn't open the door all along!! That is one of the hundred examples of great teachers my children have had!

At Ryan's school they are potty training him. Teachers are very patient with him. They also know when he gets frustrated he is going to pinch them. He pinches when he is frustrated but he comprehends what task they want him to complete. Basically, it means it is working! It takes a special person to teach a child who is special. We have been blessed to have both Redwood in Kentucky now the Opportunity School in Tiffin for Ryan's needs. I couldn't have asked for a better group of teachers if I hand picked them myself. We must all appreciate the role teacher's play in our children's lives.

NIKKI: When I was in college I took a special education class because it was a requirement for my major. "Why do I have to take this class? It's not like I'm going to teach special education or anything." HA, what's that you say about best-laid plans?

You mean everyone doesn't give every teacher and therapist gifts for every holiday? I make Halloween, Christmas, Valentine's Day, and of course, the end of the year gifts for each teacher and therapist. If I can't find the gifts I make them. My own personal therapist has a field day with that one! My sister just gave me a great idea for gifts. I just started making jewelry with beads and she suggested making a watch for each teacher and changing the interchangeable bracelet for each holiday. What do you think? Do you want to teach my children, too? Keep in mind each child has at least six teachers and therapists. You do the math. I like to acknowledge that they are my kid's "Mom away from home" and I like to thank them in my own way. Since I can't buy them real estate or automobiles, these will suffice.

46. Secretary

*One employed to handle correspondence and manage rou-
tine and detail work for a superior; or child with special
needs in this case!* (Dictionary Version and Our Version)

SANDY: Organization is one key element that helps when you have a special needs child. I of course take it "slightly" overboard with my OCD
(obsessive- compulsive disorder). Kids with special needs have a strict schedule they need to adherence. Not because it is easier for the parents or
teacher, it is the child's need. Routine is the key to helping these kids grow
and understand things better. All of us have to balance life, work, home,
budgeting, and activities. The lists are endless, especially in this day and
age. Imagine if you cannot speak, understand, or process the way other people do. Routine is what is familiar and safe. Because of this, a strict schedule is in place. It helps many special needs kids if there is a visual "picture"
schedule set up for all of the main activities in a day. This helps with their
child's transitions a lot!

Being the family's secretary can be difficult at times. Mike works many
hours outside of the home so it is my main responsibility to help keep the
flow. That means keeping everything in its place and keeping the schedule
for outside activities organized. Therapies are a major part of our life. We
are involved with occupational, speech, physical, and aquatic therapies. You
have to keep track of which time, which kid and of course which insurance.
Of course, Nikki and I joined the PTA just because we are psycho and have
nothing better to do, right? It helps on the weekends if you schedule similar activities that carry over each weekend. I say this because if there is a
three day weekend with no home structure, by Monday night your kid can
be "off the hook" if you don't stick to an organized lifestyle. If you take anything from this book, I cannot stress enough how important routine is for a
child with autism's life.

Another important organizational factor is balancing the bills and the
checkbooks. Most autism benefits are paid for out of pocket. Balancing your
wants with your needs is very important. Sometimes you have to rob Peter

to pay Paul. When creditors call on a bad month and ask when I'm paying the bill, I don't tell them the due date, I tell them the date right before the bill rolls thirty days. Sound familiar?

NIKKI: I think we de-forested the rain forest with all of the paperwork we have. All of the shelves in our kitchen are covered with our paperwork. It is my own filing system for insurance claims, artwork, bills, etc. My husband thinks I am unorganized, but I think it's just because he doesn't understand my filing process.

I save a lot of paperwork. I have old magazines, most of my children's artwork and recipes, craft ideas or articles I have torn out of magazines. I have every explanation of benefits for insurance because the insurance companies are always referring back to those when they bill us three months later. I am afraid to throw some things away- so I keep them close at hand.

I may not necessarily be a secretary; I'm more like a personal assistant when it comes to organizing my household and my children's activities. I have the paperwork, but I also have to organize the scheduling. I have to schedule doctor appointments, therapies, school functions and assessments for services. All of these appointments can take up a lot of time each week. All totaled, I can take my three kids to approximately fourteen appointments a week. That doesn't even include the field trips and extra shopping needed for food and necessities. I think the person that estimated a stay at home Mom's worth at approximately two hundred thousand dollars annually may have underestimated all the jobs we do!

47. Writer

One who writes. (Dictionary Version)

SANDY: Somehow as a kid I enjoyed English in school. English and Art were my favorite subjects. Math and I didn't get a long. It's funny now to see T.C. reading and drawing like I did as a kid. I really try to encourage Ryan to do the same. He doesn't like to sit still while I read to him, but the drawing is still coming along. One of the first things my sister-in-law and life long friend Jo gave me when Ryan was diagnosed was a journal. I probably didn't write in it enough, but some of the best material for this book was in the journal. I went back and re-read some excerpts of Ryan's journey. I was looking at notes and thoughts I had jotted down when I really took a look at the cover. It has a picture of a tree-lined road and the one word on the front is "Destiny". The front cover on the inside said these words by Thomas Merton. "Life is not a problem to be solved, but a mystery to be lived." I don't know who Thomas Merton is but I couldn't have said it better myself. Wow, how will we know what the future holds unless we live the mystery every day to our fullest capacity? We were chosen to be parents of special needs children and we were promised the ride of our life. We all need to enjoy the ride! I will continue to write in my journal, write this book and email my support community everyday for the answers I am continuously seeking.

NIKKI: I started by writing journals when I was pregnant. After that I would keep daily journals when Sean was a baby. I would write to him while I was at work crying or while pumping breast milk sitting on the toilet in the backroom of the high-end optical retail store in the mall where I worked. Run on sentence? Nah. I have journals for the girls, too, but I'm lucky if I remember to write on their birthdays, let alone the time to write everyday. I've written daily logs with my kids' teachers, too. We use them to keep each other informed between home and school. Of course by child number two, there is not enough time in the day.

113

Sean Wisor
Goodridge Elementary
January 26, 2007

Dear Mommy,

I love you. Mommy makes me feel happy. Mommy has a glowing heart filled with joy. Mommy loves Sean very much. I am so excited with mommy. Kisses from mommy make Sean feel happy. Sean loves you very much. Sean loves to go home so he can see mommy. Sean loves to be with mommy.

(Big kisses

Love,

SEAN

Sean Wisor writing a letter to his Mom, 2007

48. Allergist

A physician specializing in the diagnosis and treatment of allergies. (Dictionary Version)

SANDY: When we lived in the Cincinnati area it was part of the Ohio River Valley. People have a higher chance of having allergies there because of the pollen count and the location in the valley. When we lived there everyone in my family had allergies! We're like a barometer when it rains because everyone's sinus' get irritated. Fortunately after moving to northern Ohio most of my sinus issues have improved but T.C. and Mike's have gotten worse. With Ryan being non-verbal, we don't know how he deals with pollen allergies. Allergies can cause irritability with any kids but without him able to tell us, it makes it much more difficult!

We had some blood drawn to test if my son is allergic to casein and gluten. A lot of children with autism have a problem breaking these particular proteins down. They are wheat and dairy products. The IGE specific allergy test showed a low level or weak positive reaction for the allergen. After getting those results I figured we were in the clear for the gluten free/casein free diet. This blood test is an IGE test. To understand food allergies in these kids you need to test for an IGG allergy. Through Great Plains Laboratory we had the test done and found out he was off the charts for casein (dairy protein). He basically had the inability to break down cheese and cheese products. Milk and yogurts also wreaked havoc in his intestines. His wheat allergies and soy allergies were tested and ranged as low, but they were higher than others, like fruits and vegetables, which he will not consume by choice! We continue to accommodate his diet so his little belly isn't in pain. So far there are no indications of this but we can never be entirely sure since he can't tell us directly.

NIKKI: We're not sure how many allergies our kids have. Questions keep constantly popping into our heads. Why does Sean keep puking? Do you think he's allergic to medicine? Why does Caley get a rash from any pull-ups besides the Pampers brand?

It must be because Medicaid only carries the other brands of diapers. No really, I'm just kidding. That must be a coincidence.

One of the reoccurring problems Caley has is her reaction to sugar. Is it an allergy? She would get an itchy butt in the middle of the night and she would wake up screaming! She would wipe her butt on the carpet like a dog. Of course until we figured that out, the pediatrician suggested it may be an allergy, if not maybe she had worms. How do we know? After she fell asleep we had to use a flashlight and look into her anus to look for glow in the dark string looking worms. Sound like fun??? THANK GOD SHE DID NOT HAVE WORMS! Love is in the details.

Is Sean allergic to synthetic materials? He may be allergic or it could just be a tactile or sensory sensitivity. Why does he scream every time we put sunscreen on the kid? Does it hurt him? Does it give him a headache? Sean is a very pale boy so you wonder if his skin is much more sensitive to the chemicals in the lotion. I try to use products with no alcohol like Arbonne, or the spray kind, but he still gets upset!

49. Veterinarian

A person qualified in the science and art of prevention, cure, or alleviation of disease and injury in animals and especially domestic animals. (Dictionary Version)

SANDY: I am a dog person. Some people are cat people and others are dog people. Some can do without either. I believe it is important to grow up with a pet and bond with it, if it is in your power. I had a dog for seventeen of my first twenty years alive. Spunky was her name. I knew her most of my life, but when I went to study abroad, my parents came to visit, and told me they had to put her to sleep. I was heartbroken. Our neighbors down the street have a dog. One day Ryan and I were taking a walk and we stopped to pet the neighbors Labrador retriever. Ryan went to pet it, but pinched his fur really hard instead. Sometimes when he tickles us he pinches us so I can't be sure if it was on purpose. I don't believe he did it out of malice, he just doesn't know his strength. Those neighbors now avoid us like the plague.

When T.C. turned six, we invited his whole kindergarten class for pizza and jumping in our rented "Spider Man" house. We invited everyone in his class before we knew the loophole of inviting only certain members of the class. Evidently at T.C.'s school, if you invite one person in the class, you have to invite them all! Needless to say we had about twenty-five kids and ten parents here for the party. On that particular weekend, we had arranged to adopt a dog from a local shelter. This was planned before we knew of the party of course! We explained to the shelter my husband was allergic to long-haired dogs and that my son had autism and we didn't know how he would react to the dog. They gave us the dog on a trial basis. We brought the dog home Friday night. The Eskimo breed dog with white fur arrived in time for the thirty person, sugar high, hyper kid's party. Yes, that would be the Eskimo dog's fur that would shed at the drop of a hat! The dog was a real trooper, though. A real trooper until Ryan pulled out handfuls of fur on that poor dog. Which was worse? A husband who couldn't breathe, a bald dog, or a kid with one arm, which he would have probably lost once the dog got sick of his antics and bites it off! Needless to say if the dog stuck around it wouldn't have been fair to anyone, so we gave the dog back to the shelter. I think I'm still vacuuming up fur around the baseboards. Not all people get to be parents.

NIKKI: If I've said these things once I've said them about a thousand times. I still don't know if it's enough, though. "We don't eat dog poop, we don't eat dog food, and we don't drink out of the dog bowl!" The dogs' bowl in the kitchen can be so tempting when you have a child that will put everything in her mouth!

We probably have one of the only dogs with autism. Our dogs name is Buster. He has no spatial relation skills or any awareness of his surroundings. He also has texture and sensory issues, too. He is a picky eater and only eats certain foods, though he does have a sweet tooth. He is very kind and laid back for a pooch. The abuse that some of the kid's give him when they come to visit us is amazing. He is a great dog! The kids love him and Steve loves to rile him up and throw things in the house for him to chase! Caley will sometimes play with Buster for hours. Kiera gives him a lot of treats and feeds him meatballs right off of her fork. I know, you were thinking I didn't have enough on my plate so I rescued a dog from the shelter. Her name is Charlie. She is a girl but the kids named her. Buster needed a friend and we love dogs so I thought what the heck! Now we're all one big happy family!

50. Advocate

One that defends or maintains a cause or proposal or one that supports or promotes the interests of another. (Dictionary Version)

SANDY: I am definitely an advocate of many causes. The obvious one being autism. This fall, my niece Tiffany got married to a handsome chap named Marc. His family is mostly from France. I flew into Chicago to meet the family and to go to the rehearsal, since T.C. was in the wedding. After the rehearsal, we went to Marc's brother's home where they entertained us with appetizers and Margaritas. Well, after meeting many family members, I met an aunt from France who worked at a TV station. Her name is Francoise LaMonica. She was also an advocate for autism and taped many specials on television regarding the disorder. The only mistake, which occurred at the shindig, was nobody hung a sign that said "NO DRINKING AND PREACHING". I had the Aunt cornered and on my soapbox. I got on it and wielded a horrific diatribe of my opinions of the causation of autism, theories, cures, hogwash and therapies. I tend to become very passionate about autism, but fueled by lack of food or sleep and MANY margaritas, I had a saucer eyed, sweet little lady, cornered! Eventually, after I had sucked all of the oxygen out of the room, my sister in law recognized the deer in the headlights look on Aunt Francois' face and swooped in for the kill. She saved the day! She explained my devotion to the topic and excused us both. I avoided most of the family the next day at the wedding. I avoided them out of sheer embarrassment! I don't know if I was embarrassed because I was over served or too outspoken. That's OK, I paid for it two fold with my hang over. Score one for France!

NIKKI: I'm always giving advice to people with children with special needs. Part of my co-dependency issues, I just can't keep my opinions to my self. I offer advice when it is asked for or not. If I can help someone, I will. The autism community can be smaller than you think. Most parents who are geographically close in proximity have

119

the same doctors and therapists. Sometimes the professional can get a good feel for a parent who would be willing to help others. They will sometimes give your name and number to a parent in need. The may need to speak to a parent who has a newly diagnosed child and the already experienced parent can possibly give a little insight.

On the other hand, sometimes it seems like some of the parents who are more experienced with the issues of autism are keeping secrets for themselves, like how they got their fence paid for, or other grants and funding recourses. I tell everyone to apply for any grant I know of. Some might be saving the money for themselves. The needier you are the more worthy!

51. Holistic Medicine Specialist

One who attempts to treat both the mind and the body through natural means. (Dictionary Version)

SANDY: After Ryan was diagnosed with autism we took him to a holistic Doctor, or should I say Mike took him. He said the Doctor's bedside manner was a bit to be desired. The physician did a hair analysis on Ryan and explained his tissue mineral analysis and how his adrenal gland was functioning. He said Ryan's potassium and sodium percentage was off. The recommendations were supplements and a special diet. Ryan's hair analysis revealed there were some heavy metals in his systems, too. After out of pocket expenses, a lack of bedside manner, and a menu of dollar eating supplements we decided not to go back to this gentleman.

Another holistic medicine remedies suggested was something called a magnetic clay bath. This pulls the metals out of the body. The only problem is it can also pull out good metals needed in the body. It has the same premise of chelation. There are also supplements suggested like grapefruit extract to help aid in gastrointestinal situations and caprylic acid and garlic for Ryan's yeast overgrowth. We added probiotics to his diet whenever he was on antibiotics. Understand, most of the products you find out there you hear about through parent testimonies or you read about it on the Internet. My only advice to you is to read everything thoroughly before you try anything and know that most of these treatments can be very expensive. I am sure many families go broke trying to find the snake oil cure.

NIKKI: *We can't live without melatonin. Typical people naturally produce melatonin in their bodies, but for some reason not determined yet, it seems individuals with autism just don't produce enough to let them fall asleep on their own. Sean needs it to sleep. We finally got it after the several recommendations from Dr. Mark Deis, our beloved pediatrician. We get our stash from General Nutrition Centers (GNC). Sean takes three milligrams every night. We are lucky because he will actually chew it. It has a cherry vanilla flavor. They are sublingual which means you are* *supposed to let them dissolve under your tongue for the best results. Try explaining that to him. Like I said before, I'm just happy he takes it without any difficulty. He has not been able to fall asleep on his own since I stopped nursing him at twenty-four months, unless of course, we were in a car for twelve hours or if he was sick. My sister, Grace used to own a health food store and café. She stays current with natural healing and wellness. She is always recommending acidophilus to regulate intestinal bacteria, Echinacea to boost one's immunity, vitamins to improve overall health, mood and behavior, and of course healthy eating habits. (HA!) We did use Hyland's teething tablets that were homeopathic. She consults her Prescription for Nutritional Healing. There are so many alternative methods/therapies that are out there, but insurance companies get in the way. There is "chiropractic applied kinesiology- that works on the mind, body and spirit. There is also color therapy, light therapy, art therapy, and music therapy . . .so many choices (if you are a millionaire and can afford it why not try it). As long as you can do no harm (Hippocratic oath doctors take) why not try it? I've never been much of an experimenter and I'm less likely to try something that may endanger my child's life. Some folks out there are willing to do chelation, which is an intravenous therapy that removes heavy metals from the blood stream. From what I've read about it, children have died from this. No freaking way I am going to endanger my children in the hopes of recovering them from autism. No thanks- I'll pass! I like them just the way they are, ALIVE!*

I have drawn the line in some cases where the weird factor came into play. For example: for centuries the Native Americans use these ear candles called Indian Smudge cones. Can you guess what you are supposed to with these? The idea behind them is to remove excess earwax by are you ready? Step 1.) Put candle in ear. (OK, clearly I'm no expert but aren't candles for birthday cakes and romantic dinners?) Step 2.) Lighting the candle while in the ear. Of course the end that is not actually inside the ear because that would be dangerous. (it says this on the packaging) Step 3.) Letting the beeswax/paraffin candle burn down until it is 2 inches from the ear (what if you have really long ear hairs...YUK!!) Step 4.) Remove candle and ear wax. Yummy!!! Seriously, I have never tried this or probably will not ever try this, but the people I do know that do it, swear by it!!!!

52. Fundraiser

A person employed to raise funds. (Dictionary Version)

SANDY: I have been fortunate to have attended many fundraisers for "the cause". There have been fundraisers for the support group I belonged to in Kentucky. They had dinners and golf scrambles. I went to a fundraiser for Ryan's school, Redwood, and met a lot of the Cincinnati Bengal's football team. The coach, Marvin Lewis, actually poured me a glass of wine and talked to me for a little bit. It was fantastic! They had local news celebrities there too. It was a success.

A few years ago I had the privilege of being invited to a fundraiser in Michigan called Homes for Autism. The theme was "Out of the Shadow and into the Light." It was the 10th fund raising dinner for creating homes for autism in Michigan. It was also to help establish respite care in facilities for families in Michigan. It was amazing! My sister in law, Jo, and her husband Bruce, very generously bought my husband and I tickets to this event so we could go to a black tie affair where the proceeds went to the Autism event. Jo, who is a real go-getter, had gotten involved because of Ryan and was on the Fundraiser committee. The keynote speaker was Mark LaNeve. He is the General Motors North American Vice President of vehicle sales. One of his son's has autism. I met him and his wife Paula that night. They were so gracious and down to earth; he gave me his card and said if I ever needed anything to give him a call. I was thinking of emailing him for a new car. No seriously, I did get the opportunity to meet so many amazing people that night. It was a night Mike and I will never forget! It gave me a good example how each state's laws on autism differ from each other.

I hope to get more experience with fund raising now that I started a group in Ohio, S.A.L.S.A. is the name of the group, which stands for the Seneca Autism Learning and Support Association. We are starting a 501 C 3 charitable organization so we can raise more funds for Tiffin and surrounding communities! We are also starting a web site so people can easily access local information.

NIKKI: I am always on the look out for grants. I used to search online for Federal Grants. I don't bother looking on line anymore because you will get a gazillion fake ones that cost you money. Whose idea was that? I have applied for grants through a support group and our MRDD organization. It's not like I'm begging, but sometimes I feel like it's just short of walking around with a coffee can collecting donations like I did when I was six for the pee wee cheerleading and football team. If you are need of funding, and come on, who isn't, you need to find a local Autism Society of America chapter. They will give you legitimate advice, or point you in the right direction. It can be hard to find money and it takes a long time to fill out the applications, but it is totally worth the time and effort.

Raising children costs a lot of money. Raising children with autism can cost even more. The insurance companies don't generally pay for a lot of therapies or special schools so fund raisers may be necessary. I have heard of fundraisers for service dogs and fund raisers for organizations or schools supporting autism. Just make sure they are a legitimate organization, you don't want your hard earned money to go to someone dishonest.

53. Race Car Driver

A person who drives VERY fast to get to places on time.
(Our Version)

SANDY: Do you remember when you were young and everyone asks you those basic questions? What is your favorite color? Blue (tomboy), your favorite food? Donuts (chubby), what do you want to be when you grow up? A race car driver, No kidding! I may have learned it from my lead-footed brother Steve. He was the one who taught me to drive. I get to live out my fantasy almost every day when I am running late for work or running errands on a time schedule. I get up, shower, get dressed and get in my car to drive Ryan to school and then I drive to the park and ride and take the bus into Cincinnati. After I am off work, I take the bus back to the "park and ride", get in my car; pick out my adult music for the short drive and I pick up Ryan from school. He goes to school in the neighboring county, hence the arduous daily commute. I drive very fast to get home in time to meet the school bus in front of our home as T.C. is getting off of it. Do not factor in rain, snow or accidents, do not pass go, and do not collect **$200**. This routine is a finely oiled machine. My machine is a German engineered VW Passat. It can go very FAST. Don't worry; I'm not crazy enough to drive the one hundred sixty miles per hour the speedometer claims is the car's limit. I'm not that reckless. It is hard, though, when you are constantly on the GO and running late to therapies and appointments. We definitely live in the fast lane!

I need to heed the words by Simon and Garfunkle, "slow down, you move too fast, you've got to make the moment last."

NIKKI: *I used to say minivan drivers were bad drivers, but now that I am a minivan driver myself so I finally understand! My family and I are perpetually LATE. I am late for absolutely everything. I set my clocks ahead and something always happens right when I'm heading for the door. There is a dirty diaper, the phone ringing, the dog running away . . . anything! It doesn't help that I have to micro manage my schedule because of the sheer volume of therapies. Of course, most of the* *therapies are across town from each other, maybe that would explain my tardiness. By the time I get the kids off the bus and head out to all of the appointments I have to speed to get anywhere! I'm surprised their aren't more Mom's driving in the NASCAR series.*

54. Internet Researcher

A person navigating around the Internet for information.
(Our Version)

SANDY: When your child is diagnosed with autism it blows your mind. You don't know where to begin. You don't know if you're coming or going. You are never really prepared to hear the words spoken that your child has autism. When you see it in writing on a report it is even worse. It seems so permanent. Luckily you have the information highway out there. Anything you ever needed to know about autism is on the Internet. Anything clinical that is. It is difficult to find out what your life will be like and how long the road ahead of you will be. The Internet is a great tool to find the answers you seek. You can subscribe to many websites. I get email updates from various organizations. Cure Autism Now has a great website and they will send you updates. The Autism and Asperger Association is another website. The Autism Society of America is equally informative. All of this information is at the tips of your fingers. It only took me a long time to figure out how to use it! Back when I realized what a computer was there were one in ten thousand people diagnosed with autism. Now it's one in one hundred fifty people. Another good resource is autism related chat rooms and web sites. I belong to email groups on Yahoo for autism in Kentucky and Ohio. You get the information from other parents and you get the feel for other families' situations. It can add a lot of levity to your situation. The question is: Is your glass half full or half empty? Yes I am walking cliché! The only warning I may have about the Internet is it gives you easier access to those shysters out there. If someone is peddling an "easy" cure for autism, BEWARE. There is no such thing!

NIKKI: Search for autism, do you have a year to sort through all of the information? I looked up grants on the Internet and I got about two thousand entries. You had to buy a book to access them, so I didn't pursue it. I looked up autism on E bay and that was a gold mine. We get autism newsletters from everyone. We get updates from Cure Autism Now (CAN), Autism Society of American (ASA), and National Autism Association (NAA) and Autism Society of Greater Cincinnati. They email us with updates regularly. We also belong to a support group in Northern Kentucky (ASDN), that is the Autism Spectrum Disorder Network and its Rising Stars studios, which is a house where they hold fine arts classes for kids with autism in the Northern Kentucky/ Greater Cincinnati area. Our vitamin company emails us with updates, too. One of our favorites is Autism Link. It is like an autism search engine. We get updates from the Doug Flutie foundation and the Dan Marino organization. There are so many good organizations that will update you via e-mail.

55. Hair Dresser/Barber

One whose business is cutting and dressing hair, and performing related services. (Dictionary Version)

SANDY: Since the day our son Ryan was born we have had to cut his hair with clippers ourselves. We dressed him in dirty clothes, cleaned out the linen closet of towels and draped every part of his body so the little tickly hairs didn't irritate his face. Sometimes we cut his hair outdoors. The only problem with that is the screaming tantrum that occurs. If our neighbors didn't know us, and they didn't see what we were doing, it would sound like we were cutting off his arm. Actually it is just me, holding him down by hugging him and giving him the firm pressure he craves. Mike is the master with the clippers and Ryan is the unwilling participant. I took T.C. for a haircut and introduced Ryan to the barber. It is the coolest place I had ever experienced. It is for men and they have a big screen TV when you walk in. As you get closer to the single hair cutting stations you see there are smaller TV's at each station. As T.C. was getting his hair cut, they let Ryan sit at his own station to watch cartoons. It was a Hoot. He loved it! I did finally take Ryan to his first hair cutting appointment. We went back to the same place. I had kept my expectations so low and talked about how difficult he would be. Wouldn't you know it? He totally surprised all of us and did a fantastic job! The lady was very sweet and patient and she talked in a soft voice. The cape kept most of the hair off of him and the clippers were well oiled. That was definitely one of the problems we had. I think Mike was pulling out too many hairs with his clippers. After the woman finished she took a damp towel and wiped his face. She then finished him off with powder on his neck with a big brush for the stray hairs. He was in and out in a matter of ten minutes. He didn't even have time to get into his television show. What were we saying earlier about expectations? Sometimes, its not as if Ryan can't achieve a goal he sets out to complete, it's that sometimes I limit him too much and don't give him the chance. Something for me to work on!

On a side note, one of Ryan's teacher's names is Harriet. We love Harriet. A couple of weeks ago Ryan was hugging Harriet, but he must have been a little angry because he tried to pull Harriet's hair. The problem is, he pulled Harriet's weave off! Nobody knew she wore a weave so the kids and the other teachers' were all shocked! The teachers were laughing so hard they were ready to wet their pants! This was happening while the kids watched Ryan standing their holding Harriet's hair. I'm sure they were probably thinking "Don't make Ryan mad or he will pull all of the hair off of your head!"

NIKKI: I try to fix Caley's hair everyday, but she hates it when I brush her hair. Since we have never cut her hair before, it is rather long, but so beautiful. I usually braid her hair in pigtails, like Melissa Gilbert playing Laura Ingalls, so it doesn't knot. Who knew that hair could knot it a ponytail? I sure as heck didn't. We learned that the hard way. We talked about giving her hair to the organization "locks of love". They make wigs for kids who have lost their hair from chemotherapy. Of course we have been saying that for about a year so nobody actually believes us anymore.

I gave Sean his first haircut when he was a little over 1 year old. His bangs were in his eyes so I thought I could do it myself. He looked like that little kid from that Bugs Bunny cartoon, when Bugs filled in for the Easter Bunny. The little boy kept yelling 'I want an Easter egg, I want a Easter egg!' I think I trimmed it a few more times before I decided to get it done professionally. When Sean was about three, I took him to a children's boutique to get his hair cut, but it wasn't fun and I wanted to cry for him. He was so freaked out! He was afraid of the clippers, but they were scared to use the scissors because of his fits. They were worried he would get hurt. They suggested that we go about every two weeks so he could get used to the sights, sounds, and smells. Can I drink while waiting? Noticing a theme here?

Steve gets a hair cut at home. We have since cut Sean's hair at home, too. Also, like Sandy and Mike, we cut their hair (Sean's and Steve's) outside to help cut down on the mess. However there isn't anything to cut down on the screaming. His and ours, that is. We constructed a "magic cape" for him. OK, so it was a towel with a hole cut in it for his head but it worked for a while. We also used a vibrating hairbrush to help desensitize him to the feel and sound. That worked for a while. Now he just grins and bears it. We assume that when he's old enough to decide how he wants his hair, he'll be a longhaired- hippie freak. He'll never cut it again!

We did finally take Caley to get her haircut the weekend before she started Kindergarten. I told anyone who would listen, that we were really doing it. My friends Tracy and Angie said I had to take her to this place, I had never heard of, called "Chappies". So I called them and made an appointment for her while also explaining our unique situation that she had never ever had her hair cut, that she was five and had autism, and hated people touching, brushing, drying, or fixing her hair. I further explained that we wanted to donate her hair to "Locks of Love". When we arrived early Saturday morning they greeted us with smiles and took us to a back room where they do waxing and hair extensions. They had what looked like a dentist chair which explains why she wouldn't sit in it. No problem. Jennifer, Caley's stylist, got her a stool she could sit on. Great service! Jennifer then started a DVD for Caley to help her relax. We watched Elf; she was a bit too young for any of the other movies like Barber Shop and Beauty Parlor. Jennifer started off by cutting Caley's twelve-inch braids. I was more upset than Caley. Now with that done, Jennifer started the tedious task of combing out Caley's hair out. She was so gentle Caley didn't even know her hair was being combed. That was HUGE! You see Caley's hair was so horribly tangled from our beach vacation at Aunt Anna's, two weeks earlier. I thought I had gotten most of the tangles out. So maybe they were more dreadlocks than tangles. I had never seen her hair that bad. I tried everything to get those tangles out: leave in conditioner, sleek and shine, my twenty-five dollars Arbonne conditioner, and even Aunt Nancy's super- duper, extra strong, heavy duty conditioner. I even looked on—line and googled "knotted hair." The one suggestion I hadn't yet tried was Pam cooking spray, Yeah, that didn't work either. Nothing worked! I was terrified that when I did take her in to get her haircut they would have to shave her head. I ended up cutting tiny pieces of hair and pulling gently to get the knots out. It actually worked. I was thrilled!!! No GI Jane look. Back to the actual haircut, they treated us like royalty. They brought Caley a pink iced donut, a Popsicle, and juice. The best part of all was when Jennifer finished the cut she put glitter in Caley's hair and let her choose the color:...PURPLE. When the cut was done, an hour and half later, her hair was a bit shorter than I thought it would've been, but was fantastic!! She did cry when she saw her braids on the counter, but that was the only time she cried. They printed the "Locks of Love" certificate for and saved her hair in. They also made her a first haircut certificate to save a lock of her hair. It was an incredible experience I'll never forget. Thank you Chappies!

56. Aquatic Therapist

*One who is trained in methods of treatment and rehabili-
tation in the water.* (Dictionary Version)

SANDY: I grew up swimming. I learned how to swim at four and swam com-
petitively at six. I think some of that may have rubbed off on my kids. I
worked at the Perrysburg pool for six years. Usually when you swim com-
petitively working at an aquatic center becomes your life's work. I started as
a cashier at fourteen and worked my way up to the assistant manager in college. While I spent my summers at the pool I became certified in lifeguarding, Water Safety Instructor and CPR. What that means is I can save someone from drowning or teach them how to swim. I took a little of that knowledge and worked with my own children. T.C. is a good swimmer he's just not
a great listener. With his parents I should say. He will swim for an impartial
party, but for his MOM, not so much. Ryan is what you would call a natural.
He can hold his breath or breathe out the bubbles with no instruction. He
has very good receptive language but he doesn't really understand specific
instructions about swimming. The only problem is he has the buoyancy of a
sawed off tree stump. He also tends to get emotional if someone is swimming
in his face. What I mean is he can either be really happy and laughing or really frustrated and crying. The problem is he will continue laughing or crying
under water, too. I obviously worry about the drowning factor. I recently
started working part time. This allows me time to take both of my kids swimming a couple days a week. Swimming seems to be one of the best things for
Ryan. All of the water around him gives him the pressure he seeks, while providing freedom and movement in the pool. He can swim from one end of the
pool to the other, unaided, when he wants to. If it is shallow, though, he
chooses to bounce off of the bottom of the pool. We try to get him in the
deep end of the pool for his exercise, deep pressure, and a feeling of security in the water in case he ever jumped into the water by himself. This is so
he could navigate around a pool independently. I am not a certified aquatic
therapist, but I use the knowledge and passion I have for swimming with my
kids. I know not what the future holds but if one of my son's would become

a swimmer and I could smell that beautiful chlorine smell- well that's a good day! It is about me, isn't it?

Mike, T.C. and Ryan Hallett swimming together in Sandusky, 2007

NIKKI: We play "hardcore" when we go to the pool. We play in both the indoor and outdoor pools at the YMCA. My husband Steve does especially. He loves to play in the pool with the kids. He picks them up and puts them over his head and yells, "I'll give you a raise!" It's from the movie the" Muppet Caper". He then throws the kids in the pool with a big splash. They love it!

Sean finds his peace underwater. It's calm and quiet. It's wonderful to see the joy on his face and the true happiness he feels. I can't wait to get him to wear a snorkel and fins someday. Eventually we would love for him to try wearing scuba gear. Breathing under water might freak him out because it is so loud, but being able to stay underwater is so cool. I think a lot of children with autism find peace in the solitude of water. It seems to be very calming.

57. Crisis Interventionist

One who comes in or between by way of hindrance or mod-ification. (Dictionary Version)

SANDY: Most children with autism are very adventurous and have little or no fear for danger. My son is no different. After we first moved into our first house there was a big rainstorm. At the time, we had a sliding glass door in our unfenced backyard. We didn't really have time to meet all of the neighbors yet. I'm sure you can see where I am going with this. I went down to do a load of laundry and my then, five year old son; T.C. was in the living room with Ryan. When I came up from doing laundry I didn't see Ryan, but that isn't necessarily alarming. I just figured he went upstairs to his room. I went into the kitchen to fix dinner and told T.C. to go up and get Ryan. Just as T.C. was getting Ryan from upstairs, the doorbell rang. I went to answer the door and saw a rain soaked woman holding my son, Ryan in her arms. He was shoeless and soaked to the bone. Thank God it was summer. He had walked through the sliding glass door and closed it behind him for the first time so I had no idea the little escape artist had snuck out. He was found in the dark, in front of our house, walking down the street. My neighbor, Betsy, said it was a fluke that she was home at that time. She was putting away her groceries when she found him.

Another crisis that was averted was when Ryan was climbing the cupboards to get his fruit snacks. He slipped off and cut open his head on the corner of the kitchen island. We had to rush him to the hospital. It was the first time anything like that had happened! That child will stop at nothing to get those little tasty treats. He also loves to jump on beds. Not just jump but bionic jumping, like on a trampoline. I get so scared he's going to hit the ceiling fan or go flying off and hurt himself. No fear, I tell you. It is like the Olympics. You get these world-class athletes who master their skills. The only difference with children with autism, they also master their skills but instead of the Olympics, it's more like the X-games. They are extreme and dangerous, with no sense of fear!

NIKKI: *To diffuse a bomb you are given a warning, unfortunately there is no digital countdown to one of Sean or Caley's meltdowns. There are some warning signs, however. The stiffening of their joints or loud squeals is an indication. Why is Sean poking Caley in the eyes? My children are like Dr. Jeckel and Mr. Hyde. They are bi-polar (not really) or manic depressions, (again, not literally). Some days they all play together sweetly. Other days I have to keep them in separate rooms, or separate floors! We may get a warning sometimes, or we may just get screaming! I never had close aged siblings so this is all new to me. I called my husband; he's number three out of four boys' in his family. They are all two years apart so I consider him in expert on siblings close together. Caley was taunting Sean the one-day and I was not sure if it was the Autism Spectrum Disorder or just siblings interacting. Should I intervene? Steve basically said "kids are kids", all brothers and sisters act like this!*

58. Carpet Cleaner

A person or machine that cleans carpeting. (Dictionary Version)

SANDY: Do you want to know how my thirty-eighth birthday began? I woke up, went to work and received a call from my husband. Apparently my son Ryan woke up after I left while Mike and T.C. were still sleeping. He went downstairs to help himself to juice in the refrigerator. Instead of juice he found himself the full bottle of Hershey's Chocolate syrup. What? What is that you say? Oh yea, you knew I had already cleaned my house the previous weekend since I was having out of town guests. My husband was freaking out! He was screaming and frustrated and didn't know what to do. So what did he do? He called me. The way Mike explained it to me was Ryan was given a bath that morning and put in front of the TV in our room when he was done. He was working on T.C.'s hair since it was picture day. By the time Mike and T.C. got downstairs they found Ryan COVERED in chocolate syrup from head to toe. I believe Mike compared it to the movie "Carrie" on prom night with the blood scene! He told me how mad he was! He left the chocolate as is and he took the kids to school and went to work. I came home after picking up Ryan and wearily peered into my house. Wow, no exaggeration this time! THERE WAS CHOCOLATE SYRUP EVERYWHERE! My perception of the movie set was more like the movie "Helter Skelter!" It was like Ryan got in a fight with the syrup bottle and lost. Luckily I have my third steam cleaner I've gone through. After Oxy clean, woolite, Bissell cleaner and a steam cleaner, some of the stains came out. After three hours, I was done! I was ready to tear up the old, nasty carpeting and show off the stylish plywood underneath. Our carpeting has needed replaced for years, but there is no way I will do that until Ryan is potty trained. That is the bright side I told Mike about. The chocolate in the kitchen, den, and living room could have been worse, it could have been human feces ground into the furniture and carpeting- been there, done that! The irony of this chapter is we have since moved from our previous dwelling. What are the chances the new owners of our house in Kentucky are going to read this book?

NIKKI: Eight years ago when my sister-in-law brought a carpet steam cleaner over to my house I thought she was crazy. She had four kids, two dogs, and either two or three cats. Now I understand why she was always using it. I finally get it! It is a heck of a lot cheaper to use the cleaners you add water to and do it yourself at home than pay to get the carpets professionally cleaned four times a year. I have learned to live with the carpet stains since I have three kids and two dogs. I suppose another option could be to put down hard wood floors or linoleum through out the entire house. Maybe after we win the lottery!

A funny definition:

CARPERPETUATION (kar' pur pet u a shun) n. The act, when vacuuming, of running over a string or a piece of lint at least a dozen times, reaching over and picking it up, examining it, then putting it back down to give the vacuum one more chance.

59. Laundress

A woman who is a laundry worker. (Dictionary Version)

SANDY: If it's macaroni and cheese day put your kid in a yellow shirt. If it's spaghetti and meatball day, put your kid in a red shirt. You get my drift. The sheer volume of laundry a family of four can have is devastating at times. On any given day you can wash the clothes from three square meals and a few snacks. Then you add in towels, pajamas, outside play clothes, and soiled sheets and/or comforters- and now you have a big pile of laundry. (For just one child.) I have my work clothes, work out clothes and pajamas. T.C. has school and play clothes and Mike has work clothes and bedclothes that are size XXXLT, (which does actually take up a lot of room!) This weekend I had to wash three comforters. That is a little unusual, but it had to be done. No one likes their house to smell like urine, do they? Basically, I can spend an entire weekend just doing laundry. Each weekend there is approximately thirteen loads. Now, here comes the catch. I don't match socks. They go into a laundry basket where they sit and rot until my husband feels like matching them. They could sit there for years. We pick out socks for the day, buy new socks or wait until my husband's head is ready to explode from watching the basket sit there day after day. Don't worry. He gets even. After the plethora of laundry, someone has to put all that stuff away. I don't do socks and he doesn't put laundry away. I get around to it eventually. One day, I went to pick up Ryan at school and he was in T.C.'s pants, which are not husky, and my t-shirt. It was pretty amusing to me! I will put away T.C., Ryan's and mine, but I won't put away Mike's laundry. I can only enable so much. So by getting even, he sees how long he can live out of his laundry basket in the basement until my head explodes. Touché'.

NIKKI: I've washed everything from sofa cushion covers to phones stuck in comforters. I've also washed stuffed animals with turd on them. I just had to do that the other day! What gets out doodie? Baking soda and seltzer spot shot. Most of our furniture now has slipcovers so I have to launder those and the pillows frequently. Why don't I ever have to wash anything small? With a family of five and two dogs you can imagine the volume of laundry we have. With all of the stains we get on the clothes I have tried many different detergents over the years. Getting food stains, grass stains and kaka stains out of the clothes takes some experience. I use Tide and Oxyclean a lot. I have also used resolve pet stain carpet. My ancient Chinese secret for the laundry is Borax. You get it in the grocery store near the cleaners, not the detergents. You just put some in each load and it really helps get out tough stains. You can also put some in a bottle and it cleans the carpet.

60. Caterer

A person who provides a supply of food. (Dictionary Version)

SANDY: When preparing a meal for a child with special needs you not only need to concentrate on the child's food, but the whole family. When Ryan was on the gluten free/ casein free diet, it took a long time to balance the meal so everyone had something they liked and would eat without complaints. Sometimes it takes a miracle. The challenge is figuring out what to make that includes all four food groups, is healthy and does not contain too many preservatives or additives. To top that off you need it to be quick and easy. When you figure out what that is- give me a call! The first thing I did was buy some of those cafeteria trays. Those helped me to keep track of the different food groups. T.C. likes and eats most fruits; it's Ryan that doesn't. That does not include the gummy fruit snacks. The texture and temperature of fruit is what freaks him out. It took some time, but I realized Ryan would eat some dried fruits. Not many, but a few. I read somewhere you have to offer a child the same food 12 times and eventually they will try it. Didn't their parents tell them there are starving children in the world? I've also tried puréeing fruit and vegetables in a blender to make a smoothie. Then I got hooked on that Jack LaLane infomercial and I bought a juicer. Ask me how many times I've used that? You guessed it, not too many. Some vegetables are always going to be consumed if they are deep-fried. I don't care who you are they taste better. So, we bought a deep fryer. Do you see a pattern here? We have an appliance graveyard. Stephen King's appliance cemetery . . . Don't get me wrong, we use the basics, but I come from a childhood where I didn't learn anything about cooking. Yes my Mom was a great cook, but she wouldn't share the wealth! I had to teach myself the basics. My husband is a fantastic cook; he just isn't around long enough to prepare these great meals. I am forever buying cookbooks and trying new recipes for the kids. The challenge is getting Ryan to like the taste so much it overrides the texture. My newest problem is my kids are starving when they get home from school. We used to never eat before seven o'clock p.m. Now that I am part time my kid's tapeworms are taking over. Ryan never seems to be full. He is forever raiding the refrigerator when I'm not looking. T.C. just came in at 5:45 a.m. and explained he is starving. Starving? NONE of us are starving. Our bodies could feed off of ourselves for days. They act like there backbone is going to eat their spleen if they don't get food this instant!! To only have those problems. Remember when?

NIKKI: Back in the summer of 1992 I worked in a deli, a raw-bar and was a short order cook on the Jersey shore. What this means is making four different things for dinner never really fazes me. Although most observers think I am insane and making my life harder than necessary. We try to make a good, healthy dinner every night and eat it as a family. That never really works, though. Sean can't sit for longer than four minutes and he needs about fifteen to twenty prompts to sit down and to eat something. No one eats the same things. Steve and I could be having chili, the kids would be eating tacos, rice, meatloaf and spaghetti- dinner and life is a banquet at our house. In my next life I could be a short order cook.

61. Curator

One who has the care and superintendence of something;
or is in charge of a museum, zoo, or other place of exhibit.
(Dictionary Version)

SANDY: I love the projects kids do at the holidays. There are the ghosts made out of white paint in the shapes of their feet. There are also the turkeys they make with the shape of their hands. I love to compare the size of their hands and feet from year to year. I save most of the boy's art projects. It should only be four to five years before we need to add on to the house! In T.C.'s room I framed his first picture he ever drew that you could identify. It was a baseball mitt. We also have a project the boys made and it hangs in their bathroom. I am so proud of their projects I hang them on walls and the refrigerator. There is nothing better than a house full of original art!

T.C. is a very talented artist. My friend Jenny commissioned him to do a watercolor painting. After he gave it to her she paid him twenty dollars. She framed it and gave it to me to hang on my wall as a surprise. He was so proud of that painting. I was too!

> *"This world is but a canvas to our imagination."*
> *Henry David Thoreau*

NIKKI: I am profoundly and ridiculously proud of everything my kids create or make. I hang all of their artwork, pictures, and handprints all over the house. I hang the art on the walls, doors, cabinets, windows and shelves. Our own museum is the kid's playroom when you first walk into our house. It would normally be a family room or dining room but we converted it to hold the family's masterpieces.

(Sidebar) There is other art, though. There are sometimes fingerprints and footprint trails all over the house. Does it have to be brown? I'm not referring to muddy shoes, either. We may call that episode a: "Crapfest", "Crapisode", or a good old "Code Brown!" (This refers to feces smearing, wall covering, carpet staining and finger painting"

Picture by Sean Wisor, 2004

62. Activist

One whose doctrine or practice is that which emphasizes direct vigorous action especially in support of or opposition to one side of a controversial issue. (Dictionary Version)

SANDY: I am going to share with you a letter I sent to the fourteen board of directors of the YMCA organization in Cincinnati:

Last Thursday I attended the YMCA with my 4-year-old son and his 5-year-old brother. I decided to work out and then take the kids swimming afterwards. The plan was to drop the kids off at the child watch center for a half hour and then I would join them to go swimming. I signed both boys in, gave them their nametags, left the diaper bag and explained to the young ladies working that my son is autistic. "He is non-verbal and understands some of the things you say but not all of them." They took his coat and I left the diaper bag. When I put the nametag on Ryan I joked with the two young children watch helpers that my son would probably chew on the nametag. They suggested putting it on his back. Good idea. I put it on his back and kissed him goodbye. I left the area and went to change into my swimming suit. When I got to the locker room I realized I forgot my suit in the Child Watch Center in the diaper bag so I changed back into my clothes and went back to get it. When I went into the Child Watch area I said hello to my 5-year-old son and asked if he was having fun. He had met some new kids so of course he was having fun! I looked around for my other son but could not find him. I asked the ladies where he was and they pointed up front. "He's up there." "No, that's not him" I said. "Maybe he's in the bathroom?" "No he is not potty trained." I became very nervous and looked around the room. When I could not find him I frantically grabbed his brother and we split up and went searching the facility for my four year-old autistic son. He had on no shoes, no jacket and he cannot speak or swim. It was below 0 out that night. I knew the women could not help me look for him because they had to watch the other children, but they did not notify anyone else to help with the quest to find my son. I ran into the pool with my five year old and looked around. I saw a fireman and told him I was looking for a missing child. My older son stayed in the pool to make sure his brother didn't go in there while I continued to look in other rooms in the YMCA. He wasn't in the pool or the locker room. I peeked into the Gym but to no avail. There were parent's watching their children participating in swimming lessons. One of the Mom's saw me running around hysterically looking for my son. She ended up finding him in the corner of an exercise room near the back door. (The empty cement pool) I'm sure the door was locked for the season but the door leading to the parking lot, the woods or the door leading to Route 18 was of course open to the public." We got our stuff and started to leave when I realized what a disservice I was providing for the YMCA. If I had left without notifying anyone, nothing would ever change. 1 in every 166 kids have autism or a form of it in the U.S. Cincinnati has 20 facilities that I am sure have some children with special needs. There was a manager on duty I explained my story to. He was very honest and said he didn't really know a lot about autism or the child care center but he would take my name and number and pass on the information. The problem I am having is I don't believe in coincidence. It's not that this happened to my "autistic" son; it's that it happened to any child at all. Any child can just walk out of a child-care center undetected. There are kinks in the system that need worked out, but I am afraid that I may not have another chance to avert a tragedy. As a parent it is my sole responsibility to protect my son, but in a public facility I need the help, awareness and accountability of the YMCA to help.

Anyway, you get the gist. I wrote some more on the subject in great detail and just wanted to hear back from someone. I didn't hear back at first, which is why I sent the letter to the board. Because of the letter there was evidently a meeting. They offered free swim lessons for Ryan and some changes were implemented in the Child Watch Center. There is now a counter outside of the Watch center where everyone signs in and no one but workers and kids are allowed in there. They use an ultraviolet pen to match the parents and kids together with the nametags. The kid's nametags are also placed on their backs. The chime on the door has also been added. I commended them on their changes and the boys and me continually go to the YMCA to swim because there is no better activity for Ryan than swimming. I will add this side bar. I work out almost everyday with my friend Sheila and her kids. The ladies are awesome with Ryan now. They even put "Finding Nemo" in the DVD player when we workout so it is easier and more fun for Ryan! Thanks ladies! You rule!

NIKKI: Here is a letter I had to write concerning a picnic we attended at a local park in Cincinnati called Coney Island:

Last summer my husband's work had their company picnic at Coney Island. I wish I could say it was an enjoyable experience, but it was not! We swam in the enormous pool only to see children swimming in their underpants, not swimsuits or swim diapers. There didn't seem to be any safety precautions for sanitary reasons. Next, our then 5-year-old son, and three year-old daughter wanted to ride what my son kept calling the "Bob the builder" ride. I think it had a bulldozer. Anyway, my daughter walked right up in line and got into a car. She called for me to sit next to her. A teenager with a yardstick stopped my son with a marker on it. He told us our son was too tall to ride this ride. What? I was literally speechless and I tried to explain to my son he was too tall. I then took him to the train and boat ride, which were similar and the operator let my son right on. I then decided to go to the customer relations office and asked why my son was not allowed on the first ride which he begged to ride about a hundred times! The woman explained it was up to each operators digression as to whether or not a child who was 48" or taller could or couldn't ride their ride. My son was close to 48" in height. 47.5" to be exact! He had his six year check-up two weeks later. Did I mention my son has autism? No-

146

well it shouldn't matter but it does. His developmental age at that time was that of a three to four year old. I did not feel I should have to explain myself to a fifteen year old with a yardstick as to why my son should be allowed to ride his ride. What would have hurt to let him ride? A smile, a giggle or a grin? What a price to pay. He was "tall" enough by Coney Island standards to ride the big rides but he would have been terrified and may have tried to get out. Can you say lawsuit? The headlines would have read "Child with autism denied access to age appropriate ride and gets seriously injured as he tries to get off the Ferris wheel. Needless to say when the company picnic was again held at Coney Island we decided to go to our local pool where we just had fun. No explanations needed. So, if you have typical children who are short- take yours chances at Coney Island, but if you have a child with special needs- they're not welcome!

63. Environmentalist

One concerned with the complex of physical, chemical, and biotic factors (as climate, soil, and living things) that act upon an organism or an ecological community and ultimately determine its form and survival or the aggregate of social and cultural conditions that influence the life of an individual or community. (Dictionary Version)

SANDY: I was never a science buff because I didn't understand it very well. It is ironic that I almost didn't graduate from college because I failed Physics. Remember when I told you I was only born with the creative hemisphere of the brain? I have learned more about science as a parent then I really cared about. We live by an airport and there is a big occurrence of autism in the county we live in. When Ryan was diagnosed, my friend Pam and I were trying to find literature on a correlation between airplane fuel and special needs. Of course I have since read about environmental mercury and thimerisol in vaccines, too. Other toxins I have read about are chemicals in the water such as fluoride and second hand smoke in the air. There are so many things to read you don't know where to begin. Some of the information is government rhetoric and some of it could be a true causation for our children's health problems. Why is their one in one hundred fifty kids diagnosed with autism versus one in ten thousand kids fifteen years ago? Have our genes changed that much? I don't think so.

NIKKI: As I mentioned before I am sure we are personally responsible for deforesting the rainforests due to the mountains of insurance papers and "explanation of benefits" statements we get from the insurance companies. We get them daily! We are also to blame for global warning because I use aerosol sunscreen on the kid's because the older two hate having sunscreen put on them. Anything that is quick and safe for their skin I use. Caley has a good dark complexion and tans the second she is exposed to the sun. Kiera is somewhere in the middle. Sean ranges from pink to pale pint to blue. He was actually confused at school with the albino boy who had to wear hats outside to protect his skin. Fortunately for us Sean liked wearing hats outside every day. The school bus drivers and teachers kept sending the albino boy's hats home in Sean's backpack. Sean also has been very heat sensitive. That is because his mother is such a delicate flower. HA! I run the air conditioner from May until October. Sue me! I don't have anything to take anyway. You can have my bills or my mortgages. They are yours!!! Enjoy.

I am also a great recycler. I can find uses for almost anything! I take things that normal people would otherwise throw out and find multiple uses for them. For example, I took the clips that the kid's slippers came on and used them to hang sea life creatures from the cargo fishing net hanging from the kid's bathroom ceiling. I take foam from packing materials to make doll beds. I use water bottles one hundred times. Don't get me started on toothbrushes! I think for the five of us (seven including our dogs) I have fifty toothbrushes. I use old ones for cleaning the vacuum cleaner filter, window tracks, and around the faucets. My favorite idea was to use the giant plastic containers you get pretzels or cheese balls from the bulk stores like Costco or Sam's club. We use them for toys storage like blocks, legos or little cars. I've probably saved twenty baby wipe containers for storage of little toy characters. They are also great for pens, markers and crayons, too. Guess I am trying to make up for all of that global warming.

64. Whoopee Locator

One who navigates around the house to find a place for privacy and intimacy. (Our Version)

SANDY: "Location, Location, Location". When you live in house with two kids and they feel the need to be touching someone while they are sleeping, you: **A.**) Never have a bed alone and live like the Willy Wonka family or **B.**) Have a strained sex life. Or **C.**) All of the above. Intimacy? What's that? Go on a date? Are you kidding me? Mike and I haven't had a date, just the two of us, in years! Pathetic, yes, I know. Since we both work a lot and Mike travels some for his job, we don't get to see each other that often. When we try to find some time to be alone we are usually interrupted by one of the two dudes. We usually end up meeting in the basement. It's unfinished and cold, but private. We go downstairs to "do laundry". Understand, we really are doing laundry but we also have a side attraction. Use your imagination. To mask the noise and have complete privacy we keep the laundry on the spin cycle. We also keep one ear open for the door at the top of the stairs! It's not much, but it's something!! It also helps us keep a handle on the amount of dirty clothes before they pile up!

NIKKI: TMI? (Too much information). *I can't tell you the last time we did it in our bed. Usually we're on the floor or the sofa. (No one is ever going to come to our house again!!) Sorry Dad, Sandy started it! She made me write it! In our Master bedroom we have 2 beds we all sleep in. We have a queen size bed that Bud and Sean sleep in with his favorite sheets and then the girls and I sleep on a queen size mattress on the floor.*

"The conception of Kiera." The first time Steve and I left both Caley and Sean (The first date since first child.) We were out of town; we went back to my sister's house. All of the kids were asleep. We called from car, and my sister wanted to know why we were home so early. We had already spent the evening at "Crazy Carl's". We were playing darts and pool. We ended up having good car sex in the, minivan and "Voila"-third kid!! Welcome Kiera!

9 Months later and magic, Kiera!

65. Dentist

One who is skilled in and licensed to practice the preven-
tion, diagnosis, and treatment of diseases, injuries, and
malformations of the teeth, jaws, and mouth and who
makes and inserts false teeth. (Dictionary Version)

SANDY: T.C. and Ryan had a great dentist in Kentucky. Dr. Moore and his
brother Brian own a practice that has the ability to help children with special
needs. Dr. Moore has medical privileges at Children's Hospital in
Cincinnati. The coolest thing about the office is both kids can have their
cleaning done simultaneously, in adjoining rooms, and they are in and out.
It's so quick I don't mind taking them to the dentist. Both kids are OK about
brushing their teeth. For Ryan it is more of a sensory issue. T.C. lost his
first tooth a couple of years ago. He has already lost two more and one more
is loose. This weekend we had out of town guests and T.C. lost his front
tooth. Well, needless to say, we all went out, came home late; a "wee bit over
served" and went to bed. Well, the "world's worst parents," Sandy and Mike,
fell asleep before "instructing" the tooth fairy where the tooth was. Mike
woke up the next day and saw the saddest look on T.C.'s face. He said the
Tooth fairy forget him. OUCH. What kind of parents are we! Mike, the
quick thinking man he is, told T.C. he woke up too early because the tooth
fairy comes right when the sun comes up. I then snuck upstairs and wedged
the five spot under the sheets. We all went up together and found the tooth
fairy's money. Yea, quick thinking on the parent's part!

Now that we live in Ohio we didn't know how spoiled we were. They
don't have special needs dentists near where we live and we have had difficulties with Ryan going to the dentist. The first time we tried to introduce
Ryan to the dentist we were just going to count his teeth. He almost bit the
hygienist's hand off! We still haven't found him a dentist.

Ryan has lost a couple of teeth now. When I mean lost, I literally mean
lost. We never found them. The poor tooth fairy didn't give Ryan any
money. We never did find them! The staff at his school looked for a while
but to no avail. I didn't even know he lost his last tooth. I heard him crunch-

ing on when he was standing behind me so I told him to open his mouth. He stuck out his tongue, and there it was, his tooth! Gross!! I wonder if that's what happened to the other three? Ryan's adult front tooth has finally grown in. His baby teeth are small and adorable. They look like those little gum pieces- "chicklets." This is an impossible feat if you saw his parents' teeth. My front teeth looked like "bucky the beaver" so they had to be filed down to make them proportional to my face. Mike says he could "eat corn on the cob through a picket fence" because his teeth were so big and he had such a severe overbite. He had braces for five years. I can't even "wrap my head" around the concept of braces on a child with sensory issues!

NIKKI: As far as textures issues, Sean's are pretty quirky too. When he was around three he stopped trusting certain sippy cups. We had friends whose kids only drank milk and we had some of the same cups. I think he accidentally drank milk, or even worse, spoiled milk. He went through a period of only using sippy cups that were clean so clear so he could see the liquid, (usually only water). His next phase was only trusting green Playtex sippy cups. Those of course they stopped making. This phase lasted three years. Last summer we got him to drink from a sports cup. They were little water bottles that hold four ounces. I started him with kid's water with fluoride because of his dental problems. Our dentist- just out of dental school, almost passed out when I told him I rarely remembered to brush Sean's teeth every day AND I let him eat before bed time, IN BED!!! I would also let him snack throughout the day and drink whenever he was thirsty. I can beat myself up on a daily basis, but being this young I am still idealistic.

Do dentists have bedside manners? I think he was just out of school. Did I mention he was REALLY YOUNG? He looked at me like I was the devil incarnate! He gave me literature on the evils of letting your kid's eat before bed and drink all day long. Apparently, it doesn't matter that Sean will only drink water! All of this time I thought juice and sugar were the evils of tooth decay. Not in this case you old, stupid, silly fart I'm sure he was thinking!! He explained in way too much detail (like explaining to your grandfather how e-mail works). Anyway, I digress. The pipsqueak dentist continued to lecture me about the error of my ways and continued to explain to me how all of my children's teeth were going to rot out of their heads. Needless to say, besides the free toothbrushes, we haven't been back! We have since changed dentists and we like the new practice we're going to.

66. Hospitality Specialist

One who specializes in a particular occupation, practice, or branch of learning. (Dictionary Version)

SANDY: I love to entertain. I think it's because my parents were in a bridge club before I was born and continued to entertain with that group to this day. They would always have company over. The good thing about being a coach's wife is you get a lot of chances for entertaining. One night we had all of the coaches over after a home game. Basically, we made enough lasagna to feed an army. The team had a loss so we needed enough beverages to drown our sorrows. When I put the food out I am very anal retentive about the presentation. I put the food in the cute little matching dishes with the matching food spreaders and lay them out on the kitchen island. This, of course, is Ryan's perfect height for raiding the food. I had made an apple cake and he felt the need to sneak the first piece. I caught him before he could do too much damage, but the big hole in the cake was pretty obvious. After the night of festivities we had a couple of extra guests. Two football coaches stayed over instead of driving home after a night of festivities. The funny thing was watching the one coach waking up to look around the Buzz Lightyear bedroom. I asked him how the night's sleep was on the crinkly sounding waterproof pad on the mattress! He didn't seem to mind.

NIKKI: The satellite guy came over and asked if I ran a day care . . . well sort of. My first room in our home is a playroom, lined with toys. I think there is a primary color ABC rug on the floor. You can see why he may be confused. As for the rest of the house, no one could ever confuse me with being Martha Stewart or "shabby chic", or maybe just shabby. We have a very kid friendly home where it's OK to spill in. All of our furniture is 'hand me downs' with homemade slipcovers. Sean's computer is on a coffee table in the living room and he sits on a beanbag chair or a beach ball. Architectural Digest won't be coming to my home any time soon. We are the BEFORE picture.

SANDY: Kudos to Nikki, Steve and their family for their hospitality. I just took a road trip to Kentucky and spent four days at their house with my family. We had a blast! We went swimming at the YMCA, we "ate like Vikings" and there was plenty of movies and trampoline jumping for the kids. When it was time for us to finally leave Sean said "bye- bye Ry Ry. I started bawling like a baby. Our kids rarely acknowledge each other even if they have been in the same house together for four days. They co-exist in the same setting but they are also respectful of their own personal space and their own personal DVD players! They do like each other!

P.S. I slept on the couch and caught Sean escaping in the morning. He is so sneaky!!

67. Baker

Someone who prepares food by baking it. (Dictionary Version)

SANDY: When Ryan and I took a road trip to Virginia to visit the D.A.N. doctor it was very enlightening. We were sitting in the examination room and the doctor and nutritionist said they could smell the yeast on him. I must have been behind on the bath schedule! Yuck! They did admit the smell was very subtle. Yeast overgrowth is very common in the intestinal tract of kid's with autism. They called it "candida albicans". Upon further reading, researchers have found that many autistic individuals have a decreased number of helper T-cells that help the immune system fight infection due to genetics and environmental stimuli. There is growing evidence that the gut or intestinal tract of autism children may be impaired. To remedy the situation they put him on a medication called Nystatin. It seemed to help him. The only problem with the medication is it changes the appearance of the poop. It would pull certain fungus and yeast out. Mike and I liked to take turns changing Ryan's diaper to see what kind of wicked stuff he would excrete. I know you think that we're disgusting. It was like watching a car accident. You didn't want to look but you knew you had to take a peek out of sheer curiosity.

NIKKI: I bake when I'm depressed. It helps me keep my mind off of things. I do love to bake though. I let my four year old eat "raw" pancake batter, because it is a good sensory activity. Sometimes I may even add some raisins. At Christmas I bake at least 6 varieties of cookies because I am STRESSED. It is a very stressful time of the year for me.

I bake a lot of things; muffins, cakes, and cupcakes. One of my favorite things to do is make cupcakes for the kids' birthdays. I even bake for my friends' kids, too. When T.C. had a birthday I made cupcakes for his class, which didn't hurt since Sean and T.C. have been in the same class for four years. When I make cupcakes I either make them in ice cream cones or I let the kids frost them with their own flavors of frosting. It's a great joy to watch them have a blast in the kitchen!

One of the fun family activities we do is to make our own pizzas. The kids work the dough and I bake it. Then we spread the sauce and add our own favorite toppings. You can make one big pizza or little personal ones for each kid.

68. Car Detailer

One who cleans the details of the inside of automobiles.
(Dictionary Version)

SANDY: Have you ever seen the inside of a car after a week's vacation? It's amazing what kid's can wedge under their car seats and what they squish into the floor mats. I remember my first trip home when T.C. was younger and Ryan was a baby. T.C. was in one of those big car seats and Ryan was in the pumpkin seat facing backwards. I hated it when you couldn't see them in the rear facing infant seat. Is there nothing better than a little carsickness on formula while the other kid is eating McDonalds and I am driving? There was vomit all over my car. It took me weeks to get the barf smell out of the upholstery. After I cleaned the car out all I could smell was "Febreze!" I can't stand either smell anymore. We keep a rechargeable dust buster and one of those mini steam cleaners for the car now. The floors are moderately clean but the windows are another story. There is no glass cleaner that can clean all of the greasy fingerprints Ryan continually gets all over his windows! The lesson I have now learned it to continually clean on your trip, otherwise it will take forever at the end of the trip when you get home!

NIKKI: When detailing a car, vacuuming is just the beginning. We took a trip to King's Island and the crayons seemed to multiply. The "pukefest of 2006" fell in the summertime. It was all over the windows of the van, the carpeting, and in the vents. It happened about four hours into a twelve-hour car trip. It was about ninety degrees in early September. To add to the mess, there were melted crayons everywhere and the car seats were "crumb city". We left the car seat in the driveway because it was wet from who knows what? When we came out of the house to put the car seat back, it had ants all over it in less than an hour!!! Did I mention this was discovered when we were hoping it had time to dry and we were running late for yet another therapy session? Who has time to detail a car, anyway! Happy Days!

69. Lifeguard

Expert swimmer employed (as at a beach or a pool) to safeguard other swimmers. (Dictionary Version)

SANDY: I was a lifeguard for five years. Usually, when you are a competitive swimmer, you end up becoming a lifeguard. The skills you learn as a lifeguard can be used when you are older as you watch your own kids at the pool. This knowledge is transferable. Actually it is only transferable if you watch your child jump into the water. After we first joined the YMCA in Kentucky the boys and I went to the pool with my neighbor and her son. Ryan was still unfamiliar with pools and lakes and was not very comfortable with swimming yet. As we were unloading our gear, Ryan ran towards the pool and jumped in. Fortunately my neighbor Tonya had turned in time to see Ryan's head going under water. She screamed and pointed to the pool. I ran to the pool with my clothes on and jumped in to grab Ryan off of the bottom of the pool. I think I was way more shaken than he was. I don't think he had enough time to be scared. I did look up at the lifeguard in the chair with my panic stricken face. I said to him "My son can't swim!" His only reply was "I know." I know? Are you kidding me? I know? The dude didn't even get out of his chair. If ever I wanted to kick some booty it was then! A lot of other parents saw it and came over voicing their concerns. At least some people have compassion, eh? It was one of the scarier stunts Ryan has pulled. After that I made sure to never rely on another lifeguard to save my own kids it was my responsibility. It also motivated me to spend the whole next summer teaching Ryan to be self sufficient in water without the aide of water wings or another flotation device. He now swims with confidence, and in turn so do I!

NIKKI: I was a trained lifeguard at age fifteen. I was a lifeguard for eight years. I was even a junior lifeguard at fourteen. I've always loved swimming. With all of that training the first thing you learn is you should never go in after a non-swimmer without a personal flotation device because the swimmer can panic and take you under water with them. That rule flies right out the window when your adorable two-year-old sinks to the bottom of the pool like a rock! It explains why I can never relax at the pool. Not only am I watching my three children but the other 900 around me as well! Oh well, once a lifeguard, always a lifeguard.

SANDY AND NIKKI: On our visit to Kentucky we took Sean, Caley, Kiera, Ryan, T.C., and a family friend Kyla to the YMCA to swim. We definitely couldn't have done that without previously being lifeguards. We had a head count every two minutes. Luckily our kids didn't get out of the pool too much to go to the bathroom. GROSS! Now I know why the water seemed so murky that day! I will say the adult swim time for children with autism has got to be one of the hardest transitions every made. The guard's blow that whistle and kids must vacate the pool for fifteen minutes. We have to coax the kid's to get out of the pool! What a nightmare! Always remember bribery works. Bring a lot of food to the pool.

Ryan and Mike Hallett boating and swimming at Kelly's Island in Lake Erie! 2008

70. Landscape Architect

A person who develops land for human use and enjoyment through effective placement of structures, vehicular and pedestrian ways, and plantings. (Dictionary Version)

SANDY: My husband just informed me the other day that he never mowed the lawn the whole last football season. What does that tell you? I am the world's biggest enabler or the world's biggest sucker! I am not one of those people that enjoy working in the yard. I do not have a green thumb- I have a black thumb. The landscaping we had in Kentucky was what came with the house. I do mulch every spring but I refuse to plant new plants. I occasionally pull weeds or trim the bushes but when I get serious, "stuff happens". I was trying to kill the bugs in our weeping cherry tree so I used my bug spray on the tree. Oops, it was weed killer. I then tried to trim our bushes out front. I borrowed our neighbor's electric clippers. I cut through the electrical chord in about five minutes flat. We don't really have landscaping in our backyard-it's more like clutter. The trampoline, the swing set, a basketball hoop and a table and chairs. Now I wouldn't exactly say its "Sanford and Son's" yard, but it is no Garden of Eden, either.

Now that we moved into another house I have to start all over with the recreation equipment and planting new plants. My husband still hasn't mowed the lawn through two more seasons. I need some curb appeal but I think I will recruit my sister Kathy. She is the professional landscape architect. We installed our trampoline, now I have to plant some plants. First thing is first. I did start pulling the shrubs. It is an endless job! I bought, moved and laid out thirty bags of mulch, too. You would think I would have arms like Popeye by now. If only, there was a free landscaping fairy. I never knew how much dirt and wood chips cost!!!

We put in a new fence at our house so Ryan does not run into the street. In Tiffin, you have to have a public hearing because we live on a corner lot. Unbelievably, they needed our testimony to decide if we can put up a fence. After that, they decide if we can keep it permanently or if we have to take it down when we move. Can you believe it? The street outside of our house is like the Indy 500. When we moved here, my child hadn't been able to play in the yard because of the red tape concerning the variance for the fence. It was finally installed in the fall. Sorry about the summer you spent inside, Ryan.

NIKKI: *My sister Angela could grow orchids in the desert. Me? I could kill a plastic plant in the fish tank. I just want soft grass my kids can run barefoot through without worrying they might need a tetanus shot because they stepped on a rusty nail the builder left behind because they didn't clean up the debris before seeding the yard. Is that so wrong?? We have the worst yard in the neighborhood- dare I say the whole world. It's full of rocks, dead trees and lots of bare spots too. Under our swing set is a mound of dirt. Of course that is until it rains and then it's a mud bath. The nicest grass we have is under the deck and under the trampoline. The only fertilizer our grass has ever seen comes out of our dog. The biggest undertaking I've done with landscaping is once a year I will mulch the trees and bushes. I love the look of gardens, flowers, fountains, and koi ponds but- I don't have the money or desire to take time away from my kids to maintain a garden. I want to let the kid's go outside to play and have fun but I wanted to know that they are safe! "We all have our priorities/"*

71. Noise Control Engineer

One who exercises restraining or directing influence over noise. (Dictionary Version)

SANDY: Ryan has a tendency to cover his ears a lot. I think he is sensitive to certain sounds, unless he is just constantly trying to block us out! Sometimes when we get together with Mike's family the volume becomes loud. At holidays we can be sitting around cackling at jokes and Ryan will plug his ears. I think then it is definitely to drown us out. Some kid's with autism usually only focus on one sense intensely. For example, if Ryan is watching Toy Story and I am calling his name, he generally doesn't respond because I believe he doesn't hear it since he is so inundated with his senses already with the movie. We have had his hearing tested five times, but the doctor says it's OK. We have a stereo in our room and sometimes he'll turn it up as loud as it can go. In that instance I think it scares him more than it deafens him. Now the vacuum or steam cleaner, there's another story. He goes crazy! It's not like I'm ever steam cleaning or vacuuming, right? Wrong. He runs around plugging his ears and looking anything but happy. I have started paying more attention to what triggers his hand over his ears. It may be a sound or a frequency that bothers him. I suppose my yelling doesn't help, either, but I'm trying.

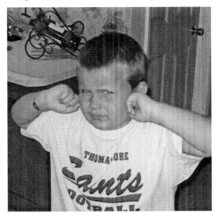

Ryan Hallett blocking out the noise, 2006

NIKKI: For some reason, if Sean's controlling the noise, it's OK. He usually plays the computer and play station two at the same time. He is OK with all of these noises, but if I try to take him into a public restroom with a hand dryer he is already running- FORGET IT! We went to an Autism Expo in Ohio a few months back and the exhibits were set up very close together. We walked in and someone was talking on a loud speaker. He wouldn't even go through the doors. Unfortunately for him, Caley thinks the louder the better. She likes everything LOUD. It could be she had bad hearing as a toddler. When she was a toddler she had sixty percent hearing loss. Now I'm worried she will do more damage to her hearing. She listens to the TV so loudly or screams all of the time. She also likes to bang on drums and pot and pans. (It makes my ears ring!)

Don't even get me started on fireworks. We actually considered going to Canada for the Fourth of July. Sean is SO terrified of fireworks he always covers his ears to protect himself from the unknown sounds. He also has auditory processing disorder (A delay, actually, he hears everything and has to filter it out what is being said to him) He takes a few extra seconds to reply to a question. We tried a listening program with him, but he kept pulling the plug halfway out of the CD player to adjust the sound coming in and out of the earphones. He's so clever! I also have to turn the radio off when I'm driving in the car and I get lost. I can't walk and chew gum at the same time, that's why I had to read and study in the quiet. My husband Steve is the opposite. He listened to music while he studied. The louder the music the more he likes it.

72. Singer

A person that produces musical tones by means of the voice.
(Dictionary Version)

SANDY: You've heard of the top forty charts? I have something called the top ten chart. Whenever I need Ryan to complete a task or calm down I have a series of songs I have to sing to get him to a "happy place". I wished I paid more attention to nursery rhymes as a kid, but my repertoire will do for now.

1. **The Alphabet Song** (with corresponding hand motions)
2. **The Itsy Bitsy Spider** (his hand over hand)
3. **Where is Thumpkin?** (he loves those fingers)
4. **5 Little Ducks** (he loves it when Papa duck sings)
5. **Row, Row, Row your Boat** (I take him hand over hand and row him really hard!)
6. **Monkeys Jumping on the Bed** (I do the telephone sign and he laughs)
7. **"You've Got a Friend in Me "**(Toy Story Theme) Need I say more
8. **Mary had a Little Lamb** (not the Andrew Dice Clay version)
9. **You are my Sunshine** (Big happy smiley song)
10. **Twinkle Twinkle Little Star** (also with complete hand motions)

We have gone to an appointment at Children's hospital and Ryan was trying to make his doctor, Dr. Manning, into a pincushion. I told her how singing calms him and she broke out in song. Her rendition of Itsy Bitsy Spider had Ryan eating out of the palms of her hand! It also worked at the emergency room when the doctor had to fix the gash on his skull. Music has saved us from many uncomfortable situations. I wonder someday if he will play a musical instrument?

NIKKI: Do you remember that family from the Austrian Alps from the movie the Sound of Music? I am an honorary Von Trappe Singer. When I am feeling depressed, anxious or stressed I listen or watch the movie "the Sound of Music". The song "I have confidence" has gotten me through some tough situations and given me confidence and courage to do the impossible on a daily basis. As a family we sing a lot of Weird Al Yankovic, Laurie Berkner, and King of Swing songs. Sean memorizes the track number and asks for the number. Mommy number six, Mommy number twelve. It's amazing! We were thrilled when the kid's started loving the "School House Rock" videos. We memorized all of those lyrics, too. We sit around some Saturday mornings and have a "jam session" together. I listen to Laurie Berkner when my kids are in the car with me. We all sing together like our "Sound of Music" family. I also listen to her when my kids aren't in the car- OOPS. It's true. . Music soothes the soul.

73. Seamstress

A woman whose occupation is sewing. (Dictionary Version)

SANDY: I cannot sew to save my life. I can tell you I have learned to mend, out of necessity, but that's all. Mike hikes his pants up when he coaches on game day. It is a nervous habit and sometimes it tears the belt loop off of his pants. I can handle that with thread and a needle but that's about it. Ryan seems to pop buttons off of his pants. I can fix those too but not very well. We keep ripping holes in our couch so I have to use one of those upholstery needles that are curved and some upholstery thread. I fix it, but I can't say it looks very good. If I have anything really difficult to sew, Mike's sister Sue helps us. She's one of those crafty people that sew window treatments and pillows. I still buy my curtains at a store, need I say more. I have no talent or patience for that kind of stuff. I can tell you if the hem comes out of my pants I have many options to share with you. You can use that stitch witchery iron on stuff, safety pins, or staples if you're desperate and at work. For jeans I just tear off the bottom and leave the hem frayed to make it look urban. Urban or lazy, not sure which! I started doing that to Ryan's pants, too! We look like twins in our jeans. Well, not exactly twins but you know what I mean.

NIKKI: My Mom and my Grandmother knew how to sew and make clothes, curtains, napkins, and more. My Dad even used the sewing machine to make repairs to his trousers. Me? Not so much. That gene skipped me along with the cleaning gene. I wish I had inherited both those skills. My life might be easier or my home would be a bit more decorated. When I think of a seamstress, I picture myself with the cloth tape measure around my neck, making costumes for school plays; leotard's for my little ballerinas or wings for the fairies.

At two years old, Sean was thirty-six inches tall and wore size four pants. Since rolling them up every five minutes wasn't an option it required some serious hemming. I'm talking five inches or more. Never in my life had I ever hemmed anything (other than crafty things or cross stitch.) I did manage to make these pants fit him. In total, there were three pairs. Now my mending pile is taller than Sean!

Thankfully, we don't do buttons, zippers, snaps, or belts! Sean's fine motor skills aren't that developed yet, although I still haven't figured out how in the world he manages to play two video game controllers at the same time. Back to hemming, Steve calls Sean's clothes consumables. We buy them cheap and he wears them until he either out grows them or they get holes in them and are thrown away. We are very lucky with the girls' clothes because our wonderful friends Nancy and Kiley have generously given us the most beautiful hand-me-downs I've ever seen.

Caley's most recent request for my sewing expertise was to make capes for her "Wonder Pets." Thankfully, I got away with no sewing at all. I just used some felt I had saved out in the garage, and matching colored hair holders. She was happy and I never had to explain why my catholic high school never offered a home economics class so her Mother can not sew a lick. I even have my grandmother's sewing machine. It makes a great table in the girls' bedroom.

74. Manicurist

A person who gives a treatment for the care of the hands and fingernails. (Dictionary Version)

SANDY: A manicurist is the last thing we could use in our house. Mike's hands are a lost cause. His knuckles are scarred from his days of playing football and he has lots of calluses on his palms. T.C. has the longest nails in the house. He hates cutting them! As a hint, I hand him my nail polish and ask him if he wants to borrow it to paint his nails. Subtle, eh? He hates that so he immediately cuts them. His nails are already caked with dirt under them. No matter how many baths we give him there is always a ton of dirt living under those things.

Ryan on the other hand has negative fingernails. He bites his nails down to a bloody stump. He has actually gotten a couple of infections on his fingers from biting them down so far. I am going to have to find something nasty to put on his hands to keep his fingers out of his mouth. Can there be anything nastier than dooty stuck in your son's cuticles or his open cuts? The sight or smell still doesn't deter him.

Back in the day I used to wear acrylic nails when I worked in the jewelry business. I no longer do that, but now, out of nervousness, I like to attack hangnails for a hobby. I am constantly chewing on my fingers and picking my cuticles. What a nasty habit. The more nervous I get the bloodier my fingers become. I wonder where my children learn these things?

NIKKI: I have to cut my children's' finger nails and toe nails while they sleep so I won't injure them. They hate getting groomed but especially getting their nails trimmed or cut. They flail about, pull, kick and scream. Sometimes it keeps me up at night wondering what lies beneath those blackened fingernails. Could it be fecal matter, ringworm, dog poop, or toxoplasmosis from the sandbox? These questions make me get up and cut them. I sometimes use a flashlight to help, - it's quite an operation. I could really use a miner's hat with an attached light or else an extra hand. I've gotten clever and put the flashlight in my mouth. Forget a nail file or emery board; my kid's hate getting anything filed! I thought an emery file would be less painful. Boy was I wrong! Sean and Caley screamed and Kiera ate the file. Go figure.

75. Doorman

An attendant at the door of a building. (Dictionary Version)

SANDY: Ryan is the gatekeeper, but I am the key master. We have added various safety features in our home. On some of our doors we have those chimes that go off if the door is opened. When a door opens in our house it sounds like you are at a store. Or you are robbing a Brinks truck. You have the choice of which alarm sound you choose.

On our back door we replaced the sliding glass door with French doors. All exterior doors have those plastic knob covers on them, too. I love it when we have company because no one can get out! Actually it's all just part of our evil plan to keep people to stay. No really I'm just kidding. We leave our garbage can in the garage so we don't have to smell dirty diapers throughout the house. One weekend we had a party so the kitchen door to the garage was more like a revolving door for empty bottles. The later people stayed and drank, the less of a chance people could work the safety doorknob cover. On top of the door we added one of those hinge looking locks, too. If you engage the lock it doesn't look like the lock could hold the door but it does. It is especially funny to watch people unknowingly try to get out!

We were up at Aunt Sue's condominium on Lake Erie. I was in the shower, Mike was on the back deck and T.C. was watching TV. When I got out of the shower I came down and asked T.C. where Ryan was. He said Ryan was upstairs. Nope, guess again. We got our search party together and tried to find the escape artist. Luckily the condo is in a gated community. I ran to the swimming pool, T.C. checked under the beds and in closets and Mike checked the parking lot. My son, who had a mouth full of fruit snacks, jumped fully clothed into the pool wearing his good night diaper. He was considerate enough to drop the DVD remote control, on the lawn chair before his jump. Thank God that little dude can swim. I should have just followed the path of fruit snacks to the pool, but I knew instinctively where he went. We have now installed door alarms and safety doorknob holders at the lake too! I don't know if my heart can take many more escapes like that. I was scared to death. On the other side of the condominium is Lake Erie. You can

171

see the bottom of the pool but you can't see the bottom of Lake Erie. We were very lucky that day.

NIKKI: I've been waiting for divine intervention on how to build a contraption that will hold a door while I push a double stroller and hold my son's hand. I imagine something out of inspector gadget or that kid from the movie "Goonies" with a device that I push a button and an arm comes out from my utility belt (thanks again Buzz Lightyear). Thankfully, someone usually will lend a hand, and thank goodness for the kindness of strangers.

I have also physically sat in front of doors trying to stop Sean from leaving. He is strong but hasn't been able to move me yet. Sometimes telling him "No" just isn't an option. It's like he forgot how to comprehend the word and nothing will stop him!

My most recent door event was I let our respite worker Kathy and her daughter Cassie in the front door. Kathy was at the house the day before and left her gym bag. So she stopped by to pick it up. She and her daughter came in and we chatted for a while then when it was time for them to leave, I followed them to the door to help them with the upper locks. You see they are vertically challenged and sometimes they can't reach the top lock. I unlocked the door and pulled but nothing happened. Hmmm? That was strange. I pulled yet again, but still nothing, so I called Steve who was upstairs with Sean and asked him to come down and help me. I thought maybe the door had swollen shut due to the extreme heat we were having. He went outside and tried to push while I pulled from the inside. Still nothing happened, except this time it looked like we might pull the door straight off the hinges. So I let Kathy and Cassie out through the garage, which normally I wouldn't let anyone in my garage because it is such a mess, my mess but still. We tried using a credit card like they always do on TV. That didn't work either. It was getting late and close to bedtime so we gave up trying to fix the door. The next day after I got the kids off to school, I called my Dad and told him what happened. His wife, Pauline, told me the same thing happened to them not too long ago and that the mechanism inside the knob had broken and wouldn't release the door. Great now how do I fix it? She said I might have to call a locksmith. I don't have money for a locksmith. We'd just keep going through the garage, thank you. My Dad confirmed that was our problem but not how to fix it. I fiddled with it for a while then gave in and called for reinforcements, my brother-in-law Blaine, the house mechanic. He has his own radio show in Philadelphia, on Saturday mornings. He gives people like me advice on house repairs and in my case how to get out of their houses. He talked me through it step by step. I got through most of it but got stuck on the actual releasing of the lock. I worked on it all day and finally got it! I was so happy!! Anything to save a buck. I ended up replacing the whole doorknob with the same one that was on our closet. Steve was so impressed when he got home. I must admit I was pretty pleased with myself too. We women can do man stuff!

76. Guilt Manager

People who cannot possibly live a guiltless life. (Dictionary Version)

SANDY: So much guilt, so little time. What can I say I'm Catholic. I'm a Christmas and Easter Catholic, but a Catholic all the same. After Ryan was diagnosed with autism I felt so guilty that it was something I did when I was pregnant. I second-guessed everything. I didn't drink any caffeine or alcohol. OK, that's a lie. I did drink once. We went to our friends; the Pauls' wedding where all of the coaches were reminiscing about the glory days, but that one doesn't count. I didn't know I was pregnant yet! After the guilt of my diet while I was pregnant I had the guilt of not being a stay at home Mom to raise my babies. I say that loosely because I now know my limitations and I may not be the stay at home type. After that guilt it was the guilt of the medications I gave my children. Should I have trusted the medical professionals? Did I give my kids too much medication or too many vaccines? Did I make Ryan's autism worse? Then there is the subject of money. Was there any way we could make more? How many therapies didn't try because we didn't have the money? How many unproven remedies did we try that made our budget too tight? Did we get too much in debt? Basically, have we done everything humanly possibly without getting a third mortgage? Last but not least the guilt about not spending enough time with Ryan. I work and he goes to after school care until three o'clock p.m. Should I be spending time for myself? Do you see what I mean? So much guilt, so little time. I'm starting to get better at letting some of that go, but in the beginning it was awful. I substituted my self-esteem for guilt. I am letting some of that go but I will probably always justify a lot of my guilt with humor and sarcasm. It's just what I do.

NIKKI: I live with consuming guilt all of the time. It's what parent's do, right?? I don't play with the kids enough during the day. The house is never clean enough. I could be doing more activities with the kids. I don't have time to exercise because I feel I need to make the time I have with them worthy. First of all, it could be because I grew up Catholic and I attended a Catholic school.

Did I eat too much tuna as a pregnant woman or while I was nursing? I've read so much about mercury in fish I wonder if that could contribute to autism. Did I take too much folic acid when I was pregnant? There is so much information out there on causation of autism but no substantial proof so we, as parents have to make up our own reasons our children are impaired. Guilt, need I say more?

77. Massage Therapist

A person trained in methods of treatment and rehabilitation in the manipulation of tissues (as by rubbing, kneading, or tapping) with the hand or an instrument for therapeutic purposes. (Dictionary Version)

SANDY: After Ryan was diagnosed with autism a parent told me about a therapy called cranial sacral therapy. This is a therapy that helps improve the fluid motion and blood flow in the body. I heard it could help some kids with autism and some kids that were born via C-Section. In some cases it is known to help children with a speech delay. Since Ryan was born C-Section and he has a speech delay and autism I figured we hit the trifecta. I signed Ryan up at the holistic health and wellness center with a therapist named Mary Ellen. She's a very calm and spiritual woman. Ryan would lie on the table and Mary Ellen would hold his head and the top of his spine simultaneously. Obviously that is where the name Cranial Sacral therapy came from! She would play soothing music, too. The room would be mostly dark and that helped Ryan to relax some. After one of Ryan's initial sessions Mary Ellen said, "He has such a large spirit, it doesn't fit in his little body." There has to be a lot of trust between the patient and the therapist. It took Ryan a few times but they definitely formed a bond. We did cranial sacral therapy for about 4 months but we had to stop because of the expense. It did seem to relax him, but unfortunately it did not unlock his speech. It was just another chapter in the book of remedies we tried to unlock Ryan's autism. I do know that to massage, stroke and add firm pressure to our children is good for Mom's and kids!

NIKKI: Have you ever tried to massage someone who has tactile defensiveness? I used to love when all of my kids were babies and I would massage them with lotion every night before bed, and after every bath. I have quite a fascination, all right obsession, with their little hands and feet. I still do if they'll sit still long enough, not squirm, and they don't scream or run away. Sean hates lotion on his body but it's ok on his feet. Our behavioral therapist Jamie says it is a good nurturing exercise but I just like doing it. I am always rubbing their backs or heads. For about a year when Sean was about 3 he would wake up with horrible leg pains. Maybe the pains were charlie horses or just leg cramps who knows? We would rub and massage his legs but we never really knew if it did any good. Believe it or not I used to be quite an athlete. Yes, cheerleading and swimming counts! But I also tried track and cross-country running. My Dad used to run cross-country so he knew how painful it could be the day after, especially if you didn't prepare properly. There were times, of course, when I would overdo it too. My Dad knew when I was in pain and gave my legs a quick rub down. His brother my Uncle Joe, was a high school football coach so he would always tell my dad techniques on how to help injuries. Sprained ankles were treated with an ice bucket and a pail of really hot water. Trust me- I was rather a klutz too, so I endured a lot of hot and cold buckets. Anyway, massages were more than welcomed, but not those buckets! I always feel I am helping my kids when I rub feet, legs and little bodies.

78. Cosmotologist

A person who gives beauty treatments. (Dictionary Version)

SANDY: The art of cosmetology doesn't really have anything to do with autism. It has to do with the amount of time autism subtracts from you getting to pamper yourself. In the amount of time it takes when you shower, a lot of damage can be done to your house. You parents know what I am talking about! I have learned to get ready in anywhere from thirty minutes down to ten minutes. Now, could I be on the cover of a magazine? Heck no! A typical day would be I wake up, jump in the shower, put mousse in my hair and go to the basement to pick out clothes for the day and throw in a load of laundry. I then pick out the boys' clothes and lay them out to dress them.

I go back upstairs, dry my hair, get the darkest make up concealer to cover the bags and circles under my eyes and throw on some eye shadow. I dry my hair, get dressed and wake the boys up. I am not raising morning people! After that we grab some breakfast and head out the door for school and work. The lipstick is whatever color I dig for at the bottom of my purse as I am driving the kids to school. Once I get to work I may reapply my lipstick but there is no guaranty. America's top model I am NOT! As the saying goes . . . "it's what's inside that counts."

NIKKI: This could go in so many different directions. Let's start with the littlest one, Kiera, who eats lipstick and thirty-five dollar bronzer. She also eats make-up, kabuki brushes, Chap Stick, and lotions. She especially likes diaper rash cream. That's one of her favorites! Thank God the lipsticks and bronzers were from Arbonne. They are non-toxic and all natural. You'll have to ask her but they must taste good, or she wouldn't keep eating them!

My son Sean likes the colors of nail polish. Sometimes he'll ask me to paint his nails. He usually wants them painted blue, yellow, and white, -a different color for each finger or toe. Caley wipes nail polish off and I'm sure the baby would eat it off her nails. Sean says "Mommy, lips" and usually touches my lips when I am wearing lipstick. All three of my children love to play with my make-up brushes. They pretend to paint the walls or brush their hair. Kiera likes to eat them. Her latest event was stealing my eyebrow pencil and coloring on the toilet, the bathroom walls, and my dresser. A few days earlier, she swiped my mascara and tried to color the bed sheets and walls. Happy days! We are never bored in our house- it's always "colorful."

79. Bartender

A person who mixes and serves drinks at a bar. (Dictionary Version)

SANDY: Another word I can think of besides bartender would be a "mixologist." I can never give Ryan just a cup of water. First of all, he is not able to drink out of a cup. He just tilts the cup back and the water flows down the front of his shirt. Second, the taste of plain old water repulses him. For a compromise, we dilute all of the juices he drinks. We do that for the taste, but mostly because of all of the empty calories in juice, too. Ryan doesn't drink milk or eat any fruit so we get calcium-fortified juices for him to drink. We also have to mix his juices and add his probiotics, enzymes or supplements. Some of his favorite concoctions have ingredients like coconut milk or highly concentrated vegetable juice. We mix his ingredients in many different ways. We have a blender wand, a food processor, a grinder, a juicer, a blender and of course a good old fashion spoon doesn't hurt! People laugh when we open his sippy cup because they just don't know what we're going to put in it. Just call me Isaac from the Love Boat! Ryan also doesn't take any medicine in pill forms so we have to mask his medication in his sippy cup too. You can never just give Ryan a sippy cup with a plain old beverage in it like you do with other kids.

NIKKI: I have made penicillin cocktails for the kids. The ingredients I use are juice, juice boxes and sprite. Sound tasty, don't you think? Caley's favorite is amoxicillin in pink milk. You mix the medicine with the "quik" powder and a little milk. Yum. Sean will not touch milk so we had to get chewable versions of the medicine and pulverize it to hide it in the chocolate pudding.

Besides the cocktails and milk, we make a mean medicine milkshake. There are "Omnicef" milkshakes and others. They're the best in chocolate because it covers the taste so well. The girl's have eaten Augmentin as a topping on ice cream with sprinkles. Anything soft and mushy generally works if you crush the medication enough. We have even tried to hide medicine in yogurt- but it never worked, but it must not have been a strong enough flavor.

80. Occupational Therapist

A person who engages someone in meaningful activities of daily life (as self-care skills, education, work, or social interaction) especially to enable or encourage participation in such activities despite impairments or limitations in physical or mental functioning. (Dictionary Version)

SANDY: My sister Sue is an occupational therapist. I have learned a lot from her and Ryan's therapists. Another great tool is the "bible" of Sensory Integration Dysfunction. It is a book called the Out-of-Sync Child by Carol Stock Kranowitz, M.A. The book gives insight into how some children process their senses and how we can cope and help kids with this dysfunction. At Ryan's school we attended an open house and I met with his Occupational Therapist Suzie. She took me into their sensory gym and showed me the things they use to help Ryan make it through a rough day. There was a platform swing, foam mats, a sensory ball, a tunnel, and a mini trampoline. The greatest thing I got from that visit is I have been listening to Ryan's needs without him speaking. Downstairs in our basement we have a remedial, makeshift gym to help Ryan when he can't go outside to play. We have a mini tramp, a tunnel, a sensory ball and a sit and spin. We also have a hammock swing and a swing that hugs you. We also keep a radio down there. He jams to his music, swings and jumps to his little heart's content. Ryan has somehow learned to "listen" to what his body needs when he gets over stimulated. He uses these tools to calm himself down . . . usually. It's called self-modulation. When Ryan is jumping up and down, stemming to "Toy Story" and running around the house like a mad man, he takes a break and jumps in the swing until it calms him down. With swimming a couple of days a week and the trampoline out back, hopefully we have enough tools to get him through a day. At his school they have a gross motor room they take him to when he is having a bad day. They also have him sit in a mini rocking chair during circle time so he stays engaged. Either the rocking horse or a therapy ball works to calm him down. I can tell you without these tools Ryan would be off the hook. In turn, I would be off the hook, too. And then Mike, T.C., and his teachers . . . you get it, the domino effect.

T.C. and Ryan Hallett on the swing in our living room, 2005

NIKKI: Don't tell Bill, Karyl, or Kim (our OT's) how we have been using our "desensitizing" brushes. We use them like surgeons to get the poop out from under fingernails, scrub turd out of carpets, clothes, sheets, blankets, and stuffed animals. I think you're getting it. As I mentioned before, Sean hates to have lotion or sunscreen put on because he is so pale, sunscreen is a necessity. They confused him with a boy at his school who is albino. His skin is hypersensitive to most elements. He screams bloody murder when we attempt to put any lotion on him. (Until recently when we discovered Arbonne's ABC baby lotion.) The secret to that one is it doesn't have alcohol in it. He still whines a bit given the day, time and mood. The brushing technique/therapy is designed to help calm them; desensitizing them to touch or grooming. Caley hates having her teeth or hair brushed. It's like trying to fight a screaming jellyfish on steroids. She is four and we have yet to cut her hair. It is very beautiful, healthy and full of golden high lights, reminiscent of our summer days at the beach and pool. Sun kissed one might say. Anyway, both kids ended up hating the brushing techniques. We might as well use the as cleaning tools. They are quite useful.

81. Detective/CSI Private Investigator

One employed or engaged in detecting lawbreakers or in getting information that is not readily or publicly accessible. (Dictionary Version)

SANDY: Sometimes when you lose something or misplace it you just chalk it up to "kids being kids" and you let it go at that. Other times, you may send out a search party for lost items or pray to St. Anthony every few hours to find the lost items. So many things get lost or moved you think you're losing your mind! How many times a day does Ryan lose a sippy cup? Twelve?? I try to find them. They're under the car seat, under the bed, in the closet . . . Now that Ryan drinks more Gatorade and diluted juices it's not as bad. I remember when he was drinking soymilk; you would find a lost cup you wondered just how long it had been under that bed. When they were gross I used to just throw them out but that became very expensive. Now I try to use the same colored cups each the day. We're down to about five cups. Gerber stopped making his sippy cups so I now I spend time investigating how to replace them through e-bay. He won't drink from any other kinds of cups. Like I said, kids with autism do not like change in their routine!

When Ryan actually feels wet he sometimes takes the initiative to pull down his wet pull-up on his own. One day he went upstairs, took off his pull-up and hid it. I suppose hiding it is better than wiping it on the carpet. Luckily it just had pee in it. He had much more interest in squeezing the mushy diaper, kneading the little squishy crystals in it and discarding it. He put a new diaper on without my help and we went to find the dirty diaper. We couldn't find it anywhere. I found it a week later in the closet. Nice.

NIKKI: My investigational skills are quite attuned to my kid's specific needs. There's the smell test, which is usually fail proof. I can smell my kid's poop from twenty feet away. I have a bionic nose. My skill for finding a lost stinky pull-up requires detective abilities. Let's see, there's the poop on the floor, the comforter and no pull- up . . . hmmm, I wonder where it could be? I found it the next day in a dresser drawer. My nose does fail me sometimes.

182

It helps to get on their level and look around. You have to check under the bed, under dressers, under the toy box . . . and sniff. Dear Watson, there is another surprise in a dirty diaper. Sometimes a "crapisode" can be camouflaged in a pattern on some materials. Whether it's a rug, clothes, or a curtain you just have to look hard enough. You have to follow the clues like "Blue's clues" and the handy dandy notebook! Remember- usually the nose knows.

82. ENT

*A person skilled in the art of healing and medicine of the
Ear, Nose Throat.* (Dictionary Version)

SANDY: You know how they say when one sense is impaired the others become sharper? None of my senses have become impaired but for some reason I think sometimes they become sharper when you're a parent. When the kids talk back under their breath, are the comments clear as a bell? Do you have new found, bionic **HEARING**? Is your sense of **TOUCH** heightened? What about your sense of **TASTE**? That's a no brainer. You put any kind of chocolate in front of my husband and me and we are in ecstasy! What about your sense of **SIGHT**? You need infrared sight on the back of your head so you can see what your kids are up to at all times. When Ryan used to drink soymilk he used to stash his sippy cup in hidden places when he was done with it. Have you ever found a nasty, old sippy cup under a bed weeks later? It's like a car wreck. You have to open it up to see what's inside! Ryan actually likes to leave the same gift at friends and families houses when we travel! Last but not least is the sense of **SMELL**. I can smell Ryan's nasty diaper the second I walk into the house. The one problem we've run into is premature changing. What I mean by that is Ryan will go into the corner and dirty his diaper. Then I'll run him to the bathroom to see if he'll go potty but we usually strike out! Then we change his diaper and right after that he will turn around and poop in his diaper again! It seems to happen every time. You'd think I would learn! It wouldn't be that big of a deal except that it's been eight years and the cost goes up as the size get bigger. I don't even want to think of the money we have spent on diapers and pull-ups. Can anyone say second mortgage?

NIKKI: Starting at age two and a half Caley had a rather bizarre habit of stuffing things up her nose like napkins, paper and rice. It was about two months that we kept smelling something disgusting on Caley. She also had a nasty smelling discharge in her diaper. We took her to the pediatrician and the Ear, Nose and Throat specialist, but they said nothing was up her nose. Yep, they were wrong! Can I get a second opinion on my mothers' intuition?? She had stuck a sticker from an apple up her nose so far, that is wasn't visible to the naked eye. That's when the Ear Nose and Throat doctor strapped her down and extracted the sticker from way up in her little nose. It traumatized her so much she almost never did it again! Periodically we have to check on her during midnight searches using flashlights and/or tweezers.

83. Interpreter

One who translates orally for parties conversing in differ-ent languages. (Dictionary Version)

SANDY: When you have a child with special needs you become an inter-preter. We went trick or treating last Halloween and I had to interpret. I pulled Ryan in the wagon with his bag of goodies. I got a good work out and he got free candy. He's a genius! Every house we went up to he would look longingly at the bowl of candy. I interpreted that as "Hey, I am a boy who loves candy, but I can't speak and I want a piece of candy!" No, really, I said trick or treat and helped him to sign "thank you" in sign language.

When Ryan wants juice he will grab your hand and steer or pull you to the refrigerator. This means he wants more juice. He also shakes an almost empty sippy cup to get our attention when he wants more juice. He just recently started pointing at things. For kids' with autism that is huge! He may also accompany that with a grunt. It gets our attention when we aren't looking at him. We are working with a communication device, too. Obviously, when he hits the icon for "drink" that is the easiest way for us to interpret what he wants, but he is just beginning with that. He is also work-ing on the sign language for drink and the sign for thirsty. His communica-tion is always improving.

Ryan's favorite pass time is walking over to the kitchen cupboard, open-ing it, pointing and grunting. At that point, I don't know if he really cares what kind of food we give him, unless of course it's a vegetable! At this stage of the game, we don't care how he communicates with us as long as he does and we can respond to his wants and needs.

His newest form of communication is squealing like a pterodactyl. Oh my gosh, you have never heard anything like this before! That is his way of telling us he's not getting his way. It is either that or it is his way of letting us know that T.C. is invading his personal space!

NIKKI: *To be an interpreter also means you need a special decoder ring. A frozen dairy treat means ice cream. Nothing is ever called its true name. It's our own language that not too many people outside of the Wisor family speak. Hence the need for an interpreter.*

When we are out at the mall or a public place and we see "one of ours" we are affectionately referring to a child or an adult who we think may be on the autism spectrum. You get to have quite a knack for picking out the kids on the spectrum or understanding the sign language or the gestures a lot of kids use. It's like most of the parents with children with autism have "autism radar". You recognize and understand the stemming and the body language a lot of these people have. Hopefully with time and more awareness other people will recognize the gestures and signs and be more empathetic to our family members.

84. Physical Therapist

The treatment of disease by physical and mechanical means (as massage, regulated exercise, water, light, heat, and electricity. (Dictionary Version)

SANDY: Ryan has something called Coxa-Valga. It's a deformity of the hip in which the angle made by the femoral neck and the femoral shaft is increased. What you probably just read was blah, blah, blah, right? Basically, it is an inward curvature of the hip that makes him more knock kneed than usual. Most kids outgrow it but some don't. One of the contributing factors can be weight. Ryan is a little above average for his age. Pardon the pun, but that's putting it lightly. Anyway, a physical therapist noticed his gait was a little unusual. He leans forward and flaps his arms when he runs. Some of that is physiological and some of that is the autism. It looks funny but that little guy has surprising speed. We take him to an orthopedist every six months because the condition needs monitored. They X-ray his hips and his knees. I initially took him to the doctor to find out if Ryan was in pain. They didn't think he was in pain so I took that information and ran with it; literally. I push Ryan to do a lot of gross motor activities. He has weak fine motor skills but he is a specimen when it comes to gross motor activities. He will be a triathlete by the time I get done training him! When we go to the park "coach Sandy" is a drill sergeant. "Walk up those ladders. Slide down that slide. Walk across that balance beam." I have him swimming and running and I recently introduced him to a bike. He can ride a big wheel all right but a regular bike is a totally different issue. It would be different if he showed any interest. I guess we just need to find his motivation. Oh, that would be food. We have to use a lot of bribery!

NIKKI: Sean started physical therapy this year. Every time he yelled- the therapist would make him do sit ups. We kept this going at home, too. Whenever he screams (in protest) he must do ten sit-ups. (I wish someone would have done that for me!) He must continue the sit-ups until he no longer yells and screams.

The kids are very physically active. They ride bikes in the neighborhood and sometimes in the house. They play on the trampoline or the swing set outside, and uses the swings in the basement. The newest addition is the scooter. It's very fun around these parts! The family that plays together- stays together.

Steve, Caley and Sean Wisor playing on their trampoline, 2006

85. Telecommunications

the *use of different means of communication such as computers, cell phones, and telephones.* (Dictionary Version)

SANDY: Support is the key for getting through the hard days for me. I started a support group in Tiffin and I keep in touch with the members via e-mail. We discuss local interventions and autism topics. Besides the autism support group our friends have our own version of a support group. My group consists of my friend Nikki, who has three kids Sheila with her three kids and some family members. We try to get together when we have the chance. We talk on the phone a few times a week. You would think we would run out of things to say to each other, but we don't. We compare notes, share great moments and listen when the other person needs to vent. We're also a group of women guilty of yelling and conversing with our children in the background during our conversation. Most people can't stand that but it has become of way of life for us. That drives my family crazy!

Thank God for cell phones. What did we do before they were invented? When I worked in Cincinnati I rode a bus home from work. I would get on the bus and usually call both ladies to see how they're doing. On the weekends we would try to get together to meet at the YMCA to work out or meet at each other's houses for play dates. Now that I moved I rely on their funny e-mail stories, our long phone calls and catching up on 'my space" or "facebook." It's a network I couldn't imagine not having. I still keep in touch with my friends from high school, college and the places I've lived. We have moved thirteen times in our eighteen years of marriage so my network of support is more like a "sisterhood: than a network. Thank God for technology!

NIKKI: I would be in the nuthouse if I didn't have a support network! Sandy, Sheila and I have a "segue-free zone". There is no warning when we are all talking to each other. It's not unusual to be speaking to one of them on the cell phone and the other one on the home phone. It's our own way of doing conference calling. Since we're all so loud it's not that difficult. We could be talking about weather, or what we made for dinner, to an article we just read, or our favorite roller coaster at an amusement park. Now how did you meet your husband? WOW. No wonder we're such creative multi-taskers. The hilarious part of this chapter is I wrote about the same thing Sandy did!!! Great minds think alike. If people sit and watch us talk to each other it can make them dizzy or give them a headache! Our kids might poop a lot but we have "verbal diarrhea"- yuk!

PHONESIA (fo nee' zhuh) n. The affliction of dialing a phone number and forgetting whom you were calling just as they answer. (Definition from unknown internet author.)

86. Book Reviewer

One who has a critical evaluation of a book. (Dictionary Version)

SANDY: I am a voracious reader. Give me <u>The Divinci Code</u> and I finished it in a day. Give me a James Patterson Novel -I've read them all. Get me a book on autism and I am slow as cold molasses. When Ryan was diagnosed I read a very good book called <u>Unraveling the Mystery of Autism</u> by Karyn Seroussi. Karyn is the Mom of a child with autism and it was written from her point of view. She gave great directions on how to treat a child with autism with the D.A.N. protocol, in which she is very active. I have begun numerous books on Autism. There are books on therapies, diets, programs, treatments and guides on how to face autism. I have also read great books where the authors have autism themselves. Their point of view is fascinating. Of course there are the books on the cured kids, which are extremely depressing because at the beginning of this journey while you're idealistic and in denial you believe that will be your child. Of course I do still believe in positive thinking and I pray some day there will be a cure, but for now, I am presently a realist. I have stopped reading too many books on autism because I have found myself in tears on too many occasions. Don't get me wrong, there are some books with great messages and I have learned ALOT from them, but for now, I can only read a little bit on autism at a time.

NIKKI: The book <u>Let me hear your voice</u> convinced me my husband was going to leave me and have an affair because I let my son eat gluten and casein in his diet! Gluten and casein are milk and wheat proteins that are virtually in almost all foods and beverages! After reading the book I felt I was poisoning Sean and giving him irreversible brain damage. I also thought that by not doing ABA (applied behavior analysis) with Sean he would never recover from autism. (Thanks- that was uplifting!) I have a real hard time reading too many books on autism because there is so much information, so little time and never enough money to support your family and try all of the special therapies that people suggest for children with autism. I'll have *to count, but when I see one book at the library that looks promising I end up borrowing about six or seven of them. I never finish any of them because I become too depressed! Hopefully people can get through this book without finding a ledge!*

87. Food Arranger/Stylist

One who hides or changes appearance of questionable food.
(Our Version)

SANDY: If you have a child that doesn't eat certain foods but they need the nutritional value, you tend to get a little devious. It can be in the presentation of the food or things you need to hide in the food. Ryan's school is equally crafty. Jenn, one of Ryan's teacher's, would hide broccoli in his cheese sauce on a baked potato. WOW. If I tried any of those three foods at home he would run for the hills. They also introduced him to refried beans, which really amaze me, considering the texture. He must trust her more than me. I hide melatonin and medicine in his sippy cup. I also get sneaky with the fruits and vegetables I put in his juice cup. Since it is opaque and Ryan can't see the liquid, he will drink it if it is sweet enough. We use a lot of V-8 and "Naked" juices that contain vegetables. I also put the gummy vitamins in with his other fruit snacks to camouflage them. When I put his dinner on the table I will put what he likes the best on top. I have been known to place french fries on a pile of chicken fingers or tortellini on a piece of garlic bread. It's all in the presentation. I may not be a great cook but I can present a heck of a meal. That's what is important, right?

NIKKI: If it does not "look right" my husband, let alone the kids, will not eat it! George Carlin once described himself as a picky eater as a kid and went on to say "is that what it's supposed to look like? Do you have a picture of that in a cook book?" Sean likes chicken nuggets (what child doesn't?) So we decided to make him pork chop nuggets with shake and bake coating on it. He loves them. Caley doesn't- but she will eat fried shrimp or fish sticks. Kiera will eat everything but Grandma Jean's parmesan chicken strip. She doesn't like the texture of the breadcrumbs. Please- if anyone else says "if they're hungry enough they will eat"- I'll kill them! My children would STARVE, literally- all joking aside, seriously! Except the baby, she would probably eat the sofa or something.

88. Waste Management

Discarded or useless material. (Dictionary Version)

SANDY: It can be embarrassing when people come over to our house and they have to throw something away. We use the two garbage cans in the bathrooms upstairs primarily for incidentals and wet diapers. The kitchen garbage cans, in most family's homes, are under the sink. Our guest's first look is under our sink. I think it's just instinct. When they realize its not there we have to explain we keep our garbage can in the garage. It is strictly for smell control. We used to keep one of those "Diaper Genies" when my kids were babies. Do you remember when those were invented? I was so excited. The boys were babies and I would throw the diaper in the genie. You would put one in the top and twist it so there was a knot in between every dirty diaper. Everything was hunky dory until you opened that puppy and years of diaper smell wafted into the air. It's like every diaper fingerprinted itself on the inside plastic and you could smell every single dirty diaper ever put in that nasty thing. I'll take an overflowing, fly infested garbage can over that any day! The cool thing with our neighborhood in Kentucky was they had garbage day *twice* a week. That rules! You would be shocked at how many dirty pull-ups we go through in a week. It's astounding. What goes in must come out. What is that saying about supply and demand? Now that we have moved to Tiffin they have a funky system for waste removal. You have to rent their can and you can only use the can for your garbage if you want them to pick it up. Once it is full you are charged for the overflow of items. We used to throw furniture and appliances away. You can only throw your garbage away. No household items or weeds from your yard. No more dumpster diving for our neighbors. We used to throw out some pretty good stuff!

NIKKI: We have three kids in diapers at the same time. My Dad bought us a diaper Genie for the last baby, Kiera. I suppose he bought it because our house must have smelled like poop. How does that saying go? "It's different when it's your own child?"

195

"Yes, well a rose STILL smells like a rose." I'm just happy when it stays IN the pull-up or diaper and not on the carpeting, clothes, sofas, walls, stuffed animals or the computer. I love the scene in the movie *"Daddy Day Care"* when Eddie Murphy goes into the bathroom after a small child goes poop. (*"Psycho"* soundtrack music is playing in the background) Eddie Murphy is HORRIFIED!

89. Locksmith

A person who makes or repairs locks and keys.

SANDY: We have one special doorknob covers on most of our doors, including our exterior doors and the upstairs bathrooms where we keep the stock pile of toothpaste. We have the kind of locks that you turn the knob and push in the whole knob and its locked. Sometimes when you want to lock them it works, sometimes it doesn't. If you want privacy, you've come to the wrong place. To unlock the doors, you have to get something long and skinny to put in the pinhole in the center of the knob. Ryan locked himself in the bathroom a couple of times and it took some time to get him out. Now we keep a wooden barbeque skewer on top of the doorframe just in case.

The big doors all have dead bolts but Ryan has figured those out. Eventually we will have to put door locks on the top of doors. We will either need a chain lock or a hotel room type lock. What is going to happen when he is taller than me? I'm sixty-four inches tall at forty and as of Ryan's last appointment he was forty-seven inches tall at seven. I'm screwed.

NIKKI: We are usually in "lock down" due to our escapes. Caley is the one who often wakes up at three or four o'clock a.m. She decides she will leave through the front door. Steve was out of town one night when she did this exact thing. I had no idea she was gone until I went downstairs the next morning to find the door was ajar approximately an inch. I tried not to think too hard of the "animals" that now may be living in our front room (playroom) we may have frogs, moles and mice but please don't let their be snakes now living in my home!!! Caley's most recent attempt could have been quite tragic. I can't let myself fall into the guilt abyss- I may never recover. She just went to explore but she came back safe. Thank God for the hotel style locks we recently installed at the top of the doors to keep the kids from leaving any more.

We were staying out of town at a relative's house over Christmas. Caley woke up. When she wakes up she is totally out of it. (Like a sleepwalker) It was four o'clock a.m. and she went up two flights of stairs calling for me and thank God my mother-in-law heard her and brought her back downstairs to the basement where we were all sleeping. She could have easily gone outside in this strange city without us even knowing she was awake, let alone wandering around outside. There are parts of my brain- dark thoughts; I just can't let myself think about. I just can't keep pondering over the "what if's."

When Kiera was about two months old, Steve was out of town. I had decided to take the kid's to the shopping mall. Santa, the big guy was coming!!! There was going to be arts and crafts, snacks, and fun for all! We had a good day and I was feeling rather- proud of myself. Then we went out to the van. (Sean was five, Caley was two and Kiera was a baby). I put Sean in his car seat and buckled him in. Then I buckled Caley in and put Kiera in her pumpkin seat. I was then going to start the car, warm it up and feed Kiera. While I was doing this I accidentally locked the car doors. When I realized this I started to FREAK OUT!!! The next logical solution was to break the window, right? I did not want to leave my babies in the car, alone, while I went to get help. My cell phone was in the diaper bag along with my car keys and my coat, which was lying next to the baby. A car drove by me at that time and it slowed down. This beautiful woman got out of her car and asked me if I was OK? Then I lost it! I started crying and told her what happened. She gave me her cell phone to call 911 and her husband got out of the car and put his coat around my shoulders and the woman hugged me. Kiera had started to cry by now and I couldn't believe how stupid I was!! What felt like forever probably was only about ten minutes. The police arrived and opened the car door. Everything was good in the world again! Lesson learned! I started wearing my keys on a ribbon around my neck, or a spare key pinned to my shirt with a pacifier holder. It's been two years and I still do this. I never want to feel that helpless again!!

90. Film Critic

One who expresses a reasoned opinion on any matter especially involving a judgment of its value, truth, righteousness, beauty, or technique of film or movies. (Dictionary Version)

SANDY: Sometimes we like to treat our family to a movie day. We go to the cheap seats at the matinee. Otherwise we go to the bank to apply for the second mortgage before going to the theatre. Have you taken your family to the movies lately? We're not the skinny family, but the butter popcorn addicted, chocolate craving, caffeine drinking family that loves to eat! We have to be VERY picky when we go to the movies because Ryan's attention span is not very long. For this reason we generally only pick animated, three-dimensional movies like Shrek, Cars, Ice Age, or Madagascar. The underlying adult humor helps us get through the movies. Another thing we do is invite our extended family and friends to go with us. Mike's two sisters like going with the boys. The Aunt's will sit through a grueling kid's movie just to watch their nephew's laugh and smile. One summer Aunt Jo and Aunt Sue took the boys to a movie while we were on vacation. It was the Jimmie Neutron movie. They say it was one of the most PAINFUL movies they ever sat through. I think that was their movie critique. Sitting, in the dark, with a theatre full of kids, hopped up on sugar in a BAD movie. Could there BE anything worse? They still talk about taking the kids to that movie. I hope they don't consider that one of the highlights of their lives? They do love to spoil the boys, though. We always have fun renting movies or going to the movies. All of our family has come to realize part of the fun in watching the videos for Ryan is the control he has of pushing the buttons and working the DVD/VCR machine. I mean come on, my sister Sue, has broken the world record for watching the movie Finding Nemo with Ryan a minimum of two hundred times. What a saint!

NIKKI: *We could learn a lot from the wisdom of movie characters. Dori, (She is the fish in the movie "Finding Nemo") said, "you can't let anything happen to him or nothing will happen to him" and "it's time to let go." "Everything is going to be all right". "How do you know?" " I don't. " Wow!*

I tried to listen to the wise words of Dori, but it is hard to let go sometimes. I drove Sean to school everyday because I was:

1. *Able to;*
2. *I wanted to;*
3. *I thought the sooner I could see him the better; and*
4. *I didn't want to spend 1 minute away from him than I had too.*

This probably explains why he was late for school three out of four days a week. When he started riding the bus to school he was thrilled! I could not believe it. I had to let him go. I could not keep him from experiencing something he really loved. I always err on the side of caution. Maybe a little too much, sometimes.

Thank you Pixar for the millions of hours of family fun!
©Disney/Pixar

91. Speech Therapist

A person trained in methods of treatment and rehabilitation with speaking. (Dictionary Version)

SANDY: Ryan has been in speech therapy since he was discharged from the state of Kentucky's organization First Steps. He gets two hours a week and his speech therapist is also working with Ryan and us with a communication device. We started him a couple of years ago on a program called PECS. It is the picture exchange program. Once the child understands the picture he can graduate up to a device. Ryan has just started working with it. He's OK. He just needs practice. Ryan is a big gesturer. There is a conundrum I have about speech therapy. How do you have a kid in speech therapy for two and a half years when he has never spoken before? I see the irony is not lost on you either. Ryan does make pretty good sounds. He also stems a little on language. He says something like "DIGGA DIGGA, TICCA, TICCA." Our friends Jenny and Todd had never heard him speak before. They were pumped when they heard him say "DIGGA DIGGA". Now when we speak to them they ask us how Digga is doing? Ryan is not the only one with speech issues. When T.C. was younger, he was also in speech therapy. He DEFINITELY doesn't have a problem with speech. Well maybe a stopping problem. He learned that one from Dear old Mom. T.C.'s issue was articulation. He couldn't really pronounce certain letters. I know some of that is age related. He still has some problems with his R's. When he gets angry with his brother he may call him Wye Wye. His speech has improved greatly, but he just lost his two front teeth so he temporarily has a "slight" lisp.

The therapists and teachers tell me promising things about Ryan's speech and his progress. They feel he may speak someday and I hold out hope for that every day. Hope is the glue that binds our family.

NIKKI: Caley has had seven speech therapists in two years. She has either burned them out or retired them. I couldn't ever give you the names of all of them. There is one speech therapist that never heard Caley speak. Remember, she is verbal. On Last

Comic Standing there was this woman with a serious speech impediment. She commented that when she was in school and had Speech therapists she had problems with *S's (lisp)*; her therapist would make her practice the word WAGON. She would stand there and repeat the word over and over. "Wagon. Wagon. Wagon." Then silence. What does that have to do with a lisp? There is no S in Wagon. She was hilarious!

When Steve was four, he would say the W sound for the R and L sound. His Mom would make him practice the sentence "rover the rascal ran for the rings." As Steve would say "Wova the wascal wan foah the wings." Is it Cindy Brady that had the **S** lisp? She used to practice "she sells sea shells by the sea shore." In choir we used to practice "rubber baby buggy bumpers" and "toy boats". Say that six times fast!!

92. Precision Repair Specialist

One who fixes something with great detail. (Dictionary Version)

SANDY: When I was in High School my parents traveled a lot. My senior year they went to Europe and I stayed home to work. Well, I told them I worked but there was a little partying on the side, too. Was that my inside head voice? In the course of my few parties,' some of my parent's travel mementos were broken on accident. We glued them together. There were many different wood animals from Africa that seemed to get broken. Several years later, unbeknownst to me, my parents had been collecting the various repaired mementos over the years. They wrapped them in a box for me for Christmas one year. I was shocked when I opened the box, because I never knew they found out about the broken wood animals! I would like to think I learned precision repair at an early age thanks to my parents.

The other day Ryan had respite care. When I got home I saw there were marks in the kitchen wall and one of my pictures in the kitchen had a broken frame. The picture sits behind Ryan's kitchen chair so I figured he must have been leaning back in is chair when the picture fell. The glass didn't break so I could fix the problem. I patched the wall and painted it. I got wood putty to fill the wood hole. I used some sand paper to smooth it and I got one of those wood markers you use for nicks in woodwork. When the wood marker didn't cover it I used a brown Sharpee marker for the rest. I also got a gum wrapper and a paper clip. Psyche! No really, the Sharpee took care of the rest and now it practically looks like new!

NIKKI: I spent many years repairing eyeglasses and eyeglass frames. For those of you unfamiliar with the process, they have tiny screws so I am used to working with small screwdrivers. A lot of the kid's toys have taken some beatings. I have taken apart many of their toys in attempts to repair them. One of Sean's favorite toys was a Dukes of Hazard, Bo Duke action figure, circa 1970. He broke it and I had repaired it. I fixed it with a paper clip and needle nose pliers, so he could still play

203

with it. He loved it! I fixed it just like MacGyver would. We have since lost it and I've tried to replace it with garage sale action figures but nothing has replaced it! So sad. In memory of the action figure I found a famous MacGyver quote for all of those thirty something parents out there!

MacGyver: "A paperclip can be a wondrous thing. More times than I can remember, one of these has gotten me out of a tight spot." *(or fixed a toy. . .)*

93. Translator

To turn from one language into another or from a foreign language into one's own: (Dictionary Version)

SANDY: The key to understanding your children is to practice. The first time T.C. started talking I couldn't understand him to save my life. I had to practice listening to him. That and Mike had to translate what he was saying to me and then I would practice with that information. I think Mike is just a better listener! That and his mouth doesn't move as much as mine. With Ryan, his teachers and I would work on using the same sign language. So far he only uses a few signs regularly. He signs mom, dad, eat, and sometimes drink, please, thank you and of course more. He has recently learned play, music and thirsty. More is the sign he uses all of the time. When you sign "more" you put all of your fingertips together and put both hands together where all of your fingertips meet. When Ryan signs "more" he actually puts his fists together. We are translating he wants more. We tease him because when you watch him sign, it's like he is telling you he wants A LOT MORE! Ryan is also working with his augmentive communication device that has picture icons on it. When he comes home he pushes the buttons to tell me how his day was. His teacher inputs his day and he translates it for me. It is so cool. He ends it by telling me if he had a good day or a bad day. He is getting better and better with it every day!

NIKKI: Sean has autism but he is verbal. He's so verbal he made up his own language for certain things. His word "stuff" is for Hershey kisses. He has many specific words for other words, too. His good night pull-ups are referred to as "a good night hassle." Is that subliminal? Sean has a new gift he has been working on all summer. He can name all cars. No two cars have the same surname. Our Mazda's name is Rex. Our mini van's name is Karen. Small cars are boys and vans are girls. It is the most amazing talent I've ever seen. Sandy's car name is Vinnie.

Caley has her own dictionary too. For Caley, the word money means "Mommy" and Da-eeee means "Daddy". We came up with our own codes, too. An ice cream truck is a music truck. An aquatic place is a pool and school time is when it's time for school. If you say to Sean "sit at the table" for a meal, he will literally sit ON the table. Sean is very good at spelling. Since he knows how to spell most words we can't be sneaky and spell out words. Now we just speak in pig Latin or certain code words.

94. Reflexology/Refluxology

To massage the hands or feet based on the belief that pressure applied to specific points on these extremities benefits other parts of the body/ the art of gagging and puking.
(Dictionary Version and Our Version)

SANDY: Ryan loves my sister Kathy. She spoils him whenever she sees him. One time when we went to visit she rubbed Ryan's feet until he fell asleep. He's been a goner ever since. Now he'll put his feet in your hands so you rub them. He likes a lot of firm pressure and rubbing. He doesn't even mind if I rub his head. Everyone likes that, don't they? When Mike and I first met that was how we knew it was true love. Both of our Moms used to rub our heads and play with our hair when we were little. I think that is one of the big reasons why we got married- so we could continue the tradition and pass it down for generations. We got engaged after only three weeks and after eighteen years of marriage I guess the head thing works!

Ryan has many food aversions. Some are because of taste and others are because of texture. On a trip to Perrysburg we were visiting my family. Mom made her famous lasagna, garlic bread and Caesar salad. We sat down to eat and Grandma voiced her concerns of Ryan's diet. She said we should have him try some salad. I explained not only is the salad green, but it is cold and wet. She said he should still try. I laid the green, cold, wet, slimy "dressed" piece of lettuce about three feet in front of him and he physically gagged. He continued to gag until we moved the lettuce out of his sight. One more second and I think her precious grandchild would have spewed all over the famous lasagna!! Should I have said, "I told you so!"

NIKKI: Reflux= puke experts. When my son Sean was a baby, my Dad put a grape on his high chair tray. He took one look at it and puked. He also watched my nephew eat barbeque spare ribs and he gagged at those, too. He is hypersensitive to the "gag me with a spoon" reflex. Now he can even gag himself.

Speaking of reflexologists . . .. I went to a reflexologist once when I was preg-nant to help me relax. - That only happened about nine years ago! I went again this summer. The therapist showed me how to find the kid's sleep pressure points on their big toes to help them relax and sleep. I think "hands on" parenting is the best, but when that doesn't work we will just resort back to melatonin!

SANDY AND NIKKI: One of our favorite stories is about Ryan and Sean. Ryan has a problem "trusting" the food in front of him so he has to feel all food with his hands and squish it between his fingers. Yes, regardless of what the food is. Sean has a texture problem, too. He gags when people are really messy and gross with their food. One year Sean and Ryan were in the same preschool. What did the teacher do? She seated the boys next to each other in the cafeteria. Ryan, the messy one, who needs to feel his food, was seated next to the habitual gagger, Sean, who sees disgusting food, pukes. So, as you can imagine, there was A LOT of gagging and puking between the two boys. Ryan changed schools the next year so that ended this "pretty picture".

95. Neurologist

A physician specializing in the medical science that deals with the nervous system and disorders affecting it. (Dictionary Version)

SANDY: I saw the following definition at an autism expo I went to with Nikki and our kids. I thought this would explain the neurology of autism better than I could: This is a definition from a woman with autism named Lynn Framer. I loved it so much I have it written on my mouse pad. Every chapter I have typed I have looked at the definition and it makes me smile! Here it goes: "AUTISM-\0-TIZ-EM\- n. A NEUROLOGICAL GLIT.C.H CHARACTERIZED BY OBSCURE TALENTS, IMPATIENCE, EXTREME SENITIVITY, DETERMINATION, FRIVOLTY & MERRIMENT, CONCEALED INTELLIGENCE, EXCESSIVE AND/OR INFREQUENT SPEECH & TORNADO - LIKE BEHAVIORS THAT MAY BE ACCEPTABLE IN A FRATERNITY HOUSE BUT NOT IN THE CHECKOUT LINE. DESPITE THESE DISTINCTIONS, INDIVIDUALS WITH AUTISM SHARE AN OCCASIONAL SMILE THAT WILL MELT A PARENT'S HEART." How does that MasterCard commercial go? PRICELESS.

NIKKI: Sean used to complain about loud noises hurting his brain. He would say, "hit your brain?" We use this expression to describe a situation when a noise or sound makes Sean's head hurt. When Sean is in control of the level of noise, he usually" cranks up" the sound as loud as possible. When he is taken by surprise by an unexpected noise, it scares and upsets him, however when he screams, it's the sound is like "nails on a chalkboard" and it hurts our heads!!

Steve's singing can be very loud at times, so it makes Sean cover his ears and cry. Caley, on the other hand, likes loud music and TV. It could be the sixty percent hearing loss she had as a baby or maybe she's just a "head-banger" like dear old Dad. Kiera doesn't seem to have a problem with loud music, either.

Have we discussed brown noise? There was an episode from "South Park," the cartoon with the foul-mouthed kids. Boys play a certain noise on the recorder and it makes people poop their pants! Steve always asks Sean, was that a brown noise? This is referring to sounds that make him cry, not poop his pants.

96. Movie Usher

Assist patrons at entertainment events by performing duties such as collecting admission tickets and passes from patrons, assisting in finding seats, searching for lost articles, and locating such facilities as restrooms and telephones. (Dictionary Version)

SANDY: When the family is brave enough to go to the movies, we spend most of the time just figuring out where we should all sit. T.C. always wants to sit in the front row. If I bring a neck brace I have no problem accommodating him. Mike is six foot, six inches tall and three hundred fifteen pounds. Besides the fact that most of the seats are uncomfortable he is considerate enough to navigate around the theatre so he doesn't block other families with his head. I don't really care where I sit; I'm there more for the popcorn and candy. Ryan tends to agree with me on this point. My only job as the family usher is to 1.) Seat Ryan between two parents so when he gets bored and tries to run we can cut him off at the pass. 2.) Keep enough variety of his favorite foods so he is focused in the theatre. C.) Most importantly don't seat him behind anyone. This is in case he is over stimulated in the movie theater and jumps up and down. It is also because he tends to kick and leg press those reclining seats in front of him whether someone is seated in the chair or not. The last time we saw a movie it was in a really crowded theater. Ryan reached for the person directly in front of him and pulled this poor man's hair. He also pinched a little kid in the row in front of him. He had never done that before. How do you explain that to another little child enjoying a movie with their family? Carefully I suppose. It can be a little embarrassing at times but I am not going to deprive my child of one of his favorite pass times in the world just to placate society. We just make sure to separate ourselves from other people.

NIKKI: The whole Wisor family went to the movies together. The only kids that attended were Sean and Caley since I was pregnant with Kiera. The local chapter of The Autism Society of Greater Cincinnati had a special viewing of Shrek two at the movie theatres in Newport Kentucky. This organization tries to do that regularly for the children with autism in the greater Tri-State area of Kentucky, Indiana and Cincinnati Ohio. In the movies they lowered the volume so it wasn't overwhelming for the children and they only dimmed the lights instead of making it pitch black. We all got a huge box of popcorn, some candy and some soda and sat down to watch the movie. The nice thing about these events is all of us in attendance were only charged the admission for the kids since the adults had to accompany them anyway. We made it about halfway through the movie. Sean had been up and down in his seat about three or four times and Caley was about the same. Steve and I sat like bookends with the kids in the middle. (How great of the Autism Society of Greater Cincinnati- kudos to them!)

* I saw these online and they made me laugh. These definitions work with all people; they just seem funnier at the movies when you are with a child with special needs!

*EIFFELITES (eye' ful eyetz) n. Gangly people sitting in front of you at the movies who, no matter what direction you lean in, follow suit. (Or jumping up and down. . .)

*ELBONICS (el bon' iks) n. The actions of two people maneuvering for one armrest in a movie theater.

97. Audiologist

A person dealing with the science of hearing. (Dictionary
Version)

SANDY: It helps to have good hearing when you are a parent. I have what
you call "Selective Hearing". It is a gift we have been passing down for generations. I sometimes use it with my children but mostly on my husband
Mike. It never fails. When I'm downstairs in the basement doing laundry
that's when everyone wants to yell for me or ask me questions that I can't
possibly hear over the sound of the washer. I come upstairs and ask T.C. what
he wanted and he always forgets. He has a really bad short-term memory
problem- or undiagnosed attention deficit, like me. While I am in the
kitchen Ryan usually sneaks upstairs. You have to keep an eye on him at all
times. The cool thing is, you can usually hear where Ryan is in the house by
the creaking of the floorboards. Of course most times he makes it obvious
because he will turn on all of the TV's upstairs, get excited and pick a bed and
start jumping on it. You can't miss that from downstairs. My favorite hearing
test is when I'm in one room and the boys are in the other and one of them
gets mad. I strain to hear what happened. Is T.C. in Ryan's face? Did Ryan
pinch T.C. while being unprovoked? Anything can happen when they get
together. Sometimes when they play together they actually laugh a lot and
no one ends up in tears. I sit back and listen to the glorious music of belly
laughing. There is absolutely nothing better than a house filled with the
sound of laughter. Laughter is the best medicine . . . for everyone!

*NIKKI: I have better hearing than a dog. I can hear my son opening up the front
door while I am upstairs in the shower. One day I heard a "cough cough" through
the baby monitor. My then one and three year girls were upstairs in the master bedroom. By the time I got upstairs Caley said, "look Mom, it's snowing!" Both girls
were covered in baby powder. (The entire bottle by the way.) Caley had this great big
smile on her face. Kiera was having fun, too, although she did look a bit confused. I
completely freaked out because I thought they would suffocate if baby powder got into*

*their lungs. (I got that mixed up with baby oil.) Either way I panicked the same. I need to **hear** them, that's why we always have the baby monitor working.*

98. Multi-Tasker

A person who can perform many tasks at the same time.
(Dictionary Version)

SANDY: To accurately portray a day in the life of a multi-tasker I am going to give the example of a weekend we are going to visit my parents. I set the alarm for five o'clock a.m. On the day we leave, if it's an ambitious day, I will throw on some workout clothes, go down in the basement, throw in a load of laundry and get on the treadmill. I will walk a mile, finish the laundry, go upstairs and take a shower. On special occasions I will take a long shower because I will grab the sickle and attempt to shave my legs. After the shower I will finish getting dressed for work, put some mousse in my hair and dry it. I then put on my makeup, head downstairs and fix my lunch. Since we will be traveling after school I will finish packing the car- whatever I didn't complete the night before. I will grab my lunch, get into my car and drive to the bus stop. Then I'll take the bus to work, work, come home and pick up Ryan. When finally home I will fill up the snack bag and fill the cooler with drink boxes, water and sippy cups. I'll "squeeze" in using the bathroom. After that I'll change Ryan and load us in the car in time for the bus to drop T.C. off. The second the school bus drops off T.C. we get on the road and trek up Interstate seventy-five to Toledo. We sing songs, watch DVD's, listen to books on tape and I do my favorite thing- talk on the phone. Most trips we drive about two hours then go through a fast food drive through and get some dinner. As I drive, I eat, talk on the phone, and give the food to the kids. I'll refill Ryan's juice and continue to be disc jockey or movie changer. When we get to Perrysburg, I change Ryan's diaper and put him in his pajamas. I get T.C. changed, hug the family and unpack the car for the weekend. It's in a days work.

NIKKI: At sixteen years old, I thought I was hot stuff because I could drive a car with a stick shift, drink a soda and smoke a cigarette. Nothing compares to what I do on a daily basis now! I have to make phone calls to therapists. I have to stay in constant contact with case works, doctors, and insurance companies. I have to take the kids to their different appointments, therapists and physicians. And you can't forget school functions. I am a room mother for my kids at school so I have to help plan the holiday parties and school activities. I also have to make time to send birthday cards to all of my family and friends and to make holiday gifts for therapists and teachers. Not to mention the everyday cooking and cleaning needed in our house. Being sixteen was "sweet" but now I know I'm a super developed time manager!

99. Author

The writer of a literary work. (Dictionary Version)

SANDY: For obvious reasons I can now put author because I have just finished my last entry in this book. That of course doesn't necessarily mean I will be a published author. No, it just means a therapeutic author. I do like to read other people's work. I am a sort of wordsmith. I collect sayings, poems and inspirational quotes and phrases. For this entry I wanted to share a passage from Sylvia Nasser, A Beautiful Mind. This was posted on our autism website in Kentucky and it stuck with me. I refer to it at times, and I hang it at my desk at work. Her it goes:

> **"Queer little twists and quirks go into the making of an individual. To suppress them all and to follow clock and calendar and creed until the individual is lost within the natural gray of the host is to be less than true to our inheritance. Life, that gorgeous quality of life, is not accomplished by following another man's rules. It is true that we have the same hungers and thirsts, but they are for different things and in different ways and in different seasons. Lay down your own day—follow it to its noon, your own noon, or you will sit in an outer hall listening to the chimes, but never reaching high enough to strike your own"** Sylvia Nasser, a Beautiful Mind.
>
> When I read this it makes the whole autism puzzle make sense. How can our four children be on the same autism spectrum but be so different from each other?

NIKKI: *I have stories going on in my head all of the time. Like that Will Ferrell movie "Stranger than Fiction"- except it seems like someone is narrating my life out loud in my head, but it's actually me. I hear things like (why is it so quiet up there)* *and then she asks knowingly, the kids must be getting in trouble; no good can come if it's quiet.*

SANDY AND NIKKI: We weren't sure where to put this poem but it is hilarious. It rhymes like a Dr. Seuss book and it is about IEP's. (An individual education plan) An unknown writer wrote it.

Do you like these IEP's?

I do not like these IEP's
I do not like them, Jeeze Louise
we test, we check
we plan, we meet
but nothing ever seems complete.
Would you, could you
like the form?
I do not like the form I see.
Not page 1, not 2, not 3.
Another change,
a brand new box, I think we all
Have lost our rocks.
Could you all meet here or there?
We could not all meet here or there.
We cannot all fit anywhere.
Not in a room
not in a hall
there seems to be no space at all.
Would you, could you meet again?
I cannot meet again next week
No lunch, no prep
Please here me speak.
No, not at dusk and not at dawn
at 4 p.m. I should be gone.
Could you hear while all speak out?
Would you write the words they spout?
I could not hear, I would not write
this does not need to be a fight.
Sign here, date there,
Mark this, check that,
Beware the student's ad-vo-cat(e).
You do not like them

so you say
Try it again! Try it again!
and then you may.
If you let me be,
I'll try again
and you will see.
Say!
I almost like these IEP's
I think I'll write 6,003.
And I will practice day and night
Until they say
"You've got it right."

We wanted to leave you with one more thought before our conclusion. On Ryan's last day at Redwood, a very special friend, Tiana, gave us a going away gift. It is a framed story by Emily Perl Kingsley. I had never read it before and it perfectly sums up everything about parenting a child with special needs!

"I am often asked to describe the experience of raising a child with a disability- to try to help people who have not shared that unique experience to understand it, to imagine how it would feel. It's like this . . . When you're going to have a baby, it's like planning a fabulous vacation trip to Italy. You buy a bunch of guidebooks and make your wonderful plans. The Coliseum. The Michelangelo David. The gondolas in Venice. You may learn some handy phrases in Italian. It's all very exciting. After months of eager anticipation, the day finally arrives. You pack your bags and off you go. Several hours later, the plane lands. The stewardess comes in and says. "Welcome to Holland."

"Holland? " you say. "What do you mean Holland? I signed up for Italy! I'm supposed to be in Italy. All my life I've dreamed of going to Italy."

But there's been a change in the flight plan. They've landed in Holland and there you must stay. The important thing is that they haven't taken you to a horrible, disgusting, filthy place, full of pestilence, famine and disease. It's just a different place.

So you must go out and buy new guide books. Any you must learn a whole new language. And you will meet a whole new group of people you would never have met.

It's just a different place. It's slower-paced that Italy, less flashy than Italy. But after you've been there for a while and you catch your breath, you look around . . . and you begin to notice that Holland has windmills . . . and Holland has tulips. Holland even has Rembrandts.

But everyone you know is busy coming and going from Italy . . . and they're all bragging about what a wonderful time they had there. And for the rest of your life, you will say "yes, that where I was supposed to go. That's what I had planned."

And the pain of that will never, ever, ever, ever go away . . . because the loss of that dream is a very, very significant loss.

But . . . if you spend your life mourning the fact that you didn't get to Italy, you may never be free to enjoy the very special, the very lovely things . . .. about Holland.

SANDY: I was having one of my daily phone conversations with Nikki when we came to the same realization. Our lives are both similar yet unique. Because of my personality and our financial situation, I chose to work full time and raise two kids with my husband. I drive to their schools and ride a bus to work each day, but the small amount of solitude I get in the car and the bus ride gives me time to reflect and think. That is part of the key to my success. Either that or it is an illusion to my success. I have also realized this is the key to me in a more nurturing role. If I take time for myself, exercise and give up the guilt, I am a better parent and wife to my family. It has taken me many years to come to this realization. By exercising more I can be more active with the boys. So, we go to the park, go swimming, play catch, or just take walks. This creates a balance that seems to work for me. Before we moved I went "part time" and it is a perfect solution for me. I get socialization from the people at work and get to use my brainpower, and then I come home, help T.C. with homework and play with the kids. I make dinner, brush everyone's teeth and we all go to bed. Done! This formula does not work for everyone. Nikki is a stay-at-home Mom. She is a caregiver of three all day long, when they are not in school. I couldn't do that. I tell her every day how much I admire her! I know my limitations.

Since we have moved to Tiffin I found out at sixteen weeks we had a miscarriage. Due to my mental health and my physical health I have opted for some time off. I am enjoying a summer with my kids but I am looking forward to going back to work part-time. Kudos to you stay at home Moms', especially the ones that home school our beautiful angels, I can only imagine how hard that is.

NIKKI: I tried to work and I don't know if it was post-partum or what- but I cried everyday for six months. We had Sean in a really expensive high quality day care for about three days. He came home with a bruise on his thigh and I lost it. He was only six weeks old and I felt terrible. I was consumed with guilt. I couldn't function being away from him and couldn't afford to not work. I was completely torn. All I wanted to do was take care of my baby. Before he was born we had it all worked out, but when it came time to leave him, I just couldn't. So I begged my sister, Angela, who was home schooling her children, Charles and William to watch Sean. Thank God, for my sanity and everyone else around me, she agreed. Steve then posted his resume on the Internet and the calls started pouring in. Two interviews later and we ended up in Kentucky where we now call home. I think I could maybe work part-time but Steve has to travel a lot and usually at unexpected times without a days notice. I would not be what you'd call "a model" employee. Sorry boss I need to take next week off because my husband's going to Ireland. Yeah, right! I used to be in management and I wouldn't hire me either. And since family is a good ten hours away by car, we don't have them as a resource. As for babysitters, we'd need three. I don't think I'd make enough money anyway. I admire Sandy for her strength and ability to keep it all together. She's alone a decent amount of the time, due to Mike's job, and working and taking care of her beautiful boys. She is a super Mom and can do it all. Most days I am in awe. You rock woman. Anyway, what was I saying? We all know our strengths and limitations. I may be a great Mom but a terrible housekeeper . . . I would rather be a good Mom.

SANDY AND NIKKI: We know that some days' it hits you harder than others. You're the parent of a child with special needs. We try not to feel sorry for our kid's and our family because what will that accomplish? I was getting dressed this morning after taking my shower when Ryan walks in and it occurs to me me; Nikki, myself and so many other parents of special needs children, rarely get a moment alone. We didn't sign up for it, but it is our lot in life. We realize we rarely get a chance to eat alone, dress alone, sleep alone or God forbid go to the bathroom alone. You parents know what I'm referring to. If we take a long shower we risk the chance of our homes being demolished by a hurricane- our children. I guess all I'm saying is; we feel your pain and frustration, your loneliness but we salute your amazing triumphs and happy times too. Each personal relationship helps to lessen the pain we may feel at times. Your personal support system, with their knowledge and awareness, is a testimony to their love for you and your children. To quote one of our kid's doctors', Dr. Manning, she said, "You seem to finally be at peace with autism." She said at the beginning we were so conflicted but that now we seem to embrace it. I suppose she is right. It can be difficult to embrace something you really don't understand but isn't that why the symbol for autism is a puzzle? Who really knows what the future holds for our kids. We will continue on this unknown journey and enjoy the ride the whole way.

While I cannot site an exact number or statistic, most articles or experts put the divorce rate for parents of special needs children at eighty percent. In this book we tell stories of our independence because our husband's are gone a lot. Mike and Steve are two of the best father's you will ever find, hands down. It is the "quality" of time they spend with their children, not the "quantity." When they walk in the door after a day at work, the children's eyes light up! I truly believe they think their dad's are "rock stars." They play, sing and laugh with the kids. The husband's still make us laugh, too. I suppose that has been a huge ingredient in the successes of both of our marriages.

It is truly amazing to me that four children diagnosed with the same disability can be so different from each other. If you learn anything from this book it is to treasure all of the little things your children give you. You learn not to take the small things for granted. You treasure that kiss, a hug, a giggle, and a glance in the eye or your child pointing at something. One of the many hard things to accept when you are a parent of children with autism is tracking their progress. All of the little things they do are miracles, but sometimes they disappear- the old "regression" trick. They may complete a milestone and go three steps forward, but then regress and go two steps back. It is probably one of the most frustrating parts of autism. You just have to wait for the next time they complete that same milestone. Whether you know someone with autism or not, hopefully you now realize there are no two kids with autism alike. They may have habits and mannerisms that are similar, but they are unique in their own right. Sean is verbal, Caley can speak, Kiera is just learning and Ryan is non-verbal. Children with autism can communicate, we just have to open up our hearts and hear their little voices. You've heard the saying, "the eyes are the windows to the soul.". Children with autism have beautiful souls as is evident when you *really* look in their eyes. The child's love and compassion can be so obvious, it's glorious.

We parents sure spend a lot of time researching . . . cleaning . . . educating . . . caring and watching . . . maybe all of us should remember to focus less on doing, and more on being. To quote the Beatles: "let it be, let it be". Kids grow up so fast-these precious children of ours, both neuro-typical and atypical, have taught us so many lessons that enrich our lives every day. We, as parents, have grown in leaps and bounds as our children grow with us; we have become *better* parents as our children have helped raised us. We hope as a result of picking up this book, you've come to the same conclusion we have . . .autism is not a death sentence; it is a *full, loving* life sentence.